BIG TROPHIES, EPIC HUNTS

A Mountain Hunter

Frederic Remington | *Ranch Life and the Hunting Trail* by Theodore Roosevelt | 1888

BIG TROPHIES, EPIC HUNTS

True Tales of Self-Guided Adventure from the Boone and Crockett Club

Introduction by Jason Matzinger
Stories selected by Hanspeter Giger and Julie Tripp
Bonus Chapter by Justin Spring

Edited by Julie Tripp

Illustrations from Theodore Roosevelt's
Ranch Life and the Hunting Trail
by Frederic Remington

A BOONE AND CROCKETT CLUB PUBLICATION
Missoula, Montana | 2014

Big Trophies, Epic Hunts

True Tales of Self-Guided Adventure from the
Boone and Crockett Club

Library of Congress Catalog Card Number: 2014946007
Paperback ISBN: 978-1-940860-03-9
Hardcover ISBN: 978-1-940860-09-1
e-ISBN: 978-1-940860-04-6
Published August 2014

Published in the United States of America by the
Boone and Crockett Club
250 Station Drive, Missoula, Montana 59801
Phone (406) 542-1888
Fax (406) 542-0784
Toll-Free (888) 840-4868 (book orders only)
www.boone-crockett.org

Printed in the U.S.A.

Contents

Introduction

THERE'S NOTHING BETTER THAN THE FEELING OF KNOWING YOU hunted as hard as you possibly could. Whether it's a successful hunt or an unsuccessful one, knowing you gave it everything you could is satisfaction in itself.

Some of my most memorable hunts were the ones that I never punched a tag on, but was physically exhausted at the end of the hunt. When I look at the heads and hides on my wall, every one of them has a memory that I will cherish forever. However it's the ones that I researched the area, planned the hunt, stuck to my plan, and came home with a full cooler that mean the very most to me.

If hunting was only about the kill, I don't know a single person who would be as dedicated and passionate about the sport. I'm not sure any of us would hunt at all? It's that challenge and not knowing how it will end that pushes us to get up earlier, hike harder, and hunt smarter.

Hunting has never been easy but it's what has kept mankind alive and thriving since humans roamed this earth. It's what has kept our wildlife in healthy numbers that continue to grow year after year. I truly believe that the only way hunting will be around for our grandchildren to enjoy is by sticking to everything that fair chase hunting represents. Ethical, sportsmanlike pursuit of free-ranging wild, native North American big game.

Hunt Hard,
Jason Matzinger
Hunter & Filmmaker
Into High Country

Sagamore Hill Award Winners

Created in 1948, the Sagamore Hill Medal is given by the Boone and Crockett Club in conjunction with the Roosevelt family in memory of Theodore Roosevelt (founder and first president of B&C), and his sons, Theodore Roosevelt, Jr., and Kermit Roosevelt. It may be awarded by a B&C Big Game Awards Judges Panel, if they believe there is an outstanding trophy worthy of great distinction. The Sagamore Hill Medal is the highest award given by B&C, and the following chapter includes the stories of many of these award-winning hunts.

WORLD RECORD
BROWN BEAR
KILLED BY BOB REEVE
OWNER-OPERATOR
REEVE ALEUTIAN AIRWAYS

ANCHORAGE HUNTER AND
of an 1,800-pound Alaska brown bear he shot las

By ALICE FREIN JOHNSON
Times Staff Correspondent

WASHINGTON, Jan. 29.— When Robert Reeve, Anchorage flyer, shot an 1,800-pound Alaska brown bear last May, he knew it was a big fellow, but he didn't realize it would set a world record.

Reeve was awarded a bronze medal and certificate for the bear record at the recent annual meeting of the Boone and Crockett Club, held in the American Museum of Natural History, New York. He was the only North American hunter to establish a world record in 1948, second year the club has held hunting competitions.

As further recognition of his feat, Reeve learned here this

a special medal in honor of his achievement.

Would Have Weighed More

The flyer-sportsman, head of the firm which delivers air mail to the Aleutians, said he shot the bear May 26 near Cold Bay, at the tip of the Alaska Peninsula, soon after the beast had emerged from hibernation — hungry and mean. Had it been shot near the end of its normal salmon-eating season, Reeve estimated it would have weighed about 2,200 pounds.

The bear's pelt is 12 feet 4 inches wide and 10 feet 4 inches long. Its skull-basis for determining records—is 19 3/16 inches by 11½ inches, or 1/16 of an inch longer than that of the former record bear.

Shoulder height of Reeve's bear

erect. It wa
96 Winchester.

Planned Hunting

Boone and Crocke
petitions, open to a
ican hunters, are
ulate greater
among hunters thr
hunting."

Thirty-four hun
1948 medals an
In addition to Ree
the Pacific Northw
were:

D. S. Hopkins, S
award for stone sh
of British Columb
O. D. Halsten, Si
T. A. Wharton, A
white sheep; and
Atkinson, Fort R
Alaska brown be

The Sagamore Hill Award

Hanspeter Giger

B&C Lifetime Associate and Official Measurer

SOME OF US ARE *DREAMERS*, IN ADMIRATION—OCCASIONALLY IN awe—of the *doers* of the world. The challenges of life, the prioritization of making ends meet and satisfying the needs of others, often trump the pursuit of our own childhood dreams. Still, we humans are perpetually capable of changing course, adapting, and making things happen. Doers (large and small) in this sense are the very few who manage to squeeze more drops out of this brief existence—whether it be through greatness, some notable achievement, or more often through good deeds and memories shared. Their stories lend perspective, community, inspiration, and motivation to others.

Through brilliance, vision, hard work, inner drive, or just some really good decisions, in these doers we can expect to find much in terms of sacrifice—and failure as well. These elements are often the stumbling blocks of *mere* dreamers. The doers maintain a certain spark and do not give up. Often, it's in the taking of the obscure tributary, the path of great resistance to a highly uncertain outcome

The first Sagamore Hill Medal went to Alaskan Robert Reeve for his impressive Alaska brown bear taken in 1948.

[11]

that we truly challenge ourselves. At times, even us dreamers experience and achieve greater things than our vast imaginations conjure up along the way.

Because of this, dreamers can always be reminded of possibilities—of alternative outcomes—that may be even better than our dream scenarios. Doers tend to take on the risks and low probabilities because of, rather than in spite of, these uncertain outcomes and potential failures. Further, humans own the power of the narrative, and in that the potential for great inspiration as well.

Perhaps for the non-sheep hunter, it is in the tales of mental stamina and sheer determination, the physical challenges and frequently extreme conditions, and the truly rarified air and surrealistic landscapes of the domain of the wild sheep of the world that we are awakened and challenged to think bigger and do more. The story, or just the image, of the grizzled hunter with a hard-won ram can re-ignite the pilot light of our individual dreams—for hunters and non-hunters alike.

We're all dreamers *and* doers in our own lives and circumstances. Further, we can always be inspired to expand our horizons and explore beyond our physical or psychological boundaries. Heck, even this kid once drew full-curl rams and sculpted them from clay. Maybe he can still climb a mountain and see the sheep from afar in some vast and isolated high country wilderness. That would be a start—possibilities and inspiration!

A Brief History of the Sagamore Hill Award
As noted on the Boone and Crockett Club's website:

> *The Sagamore Hill Medal is given by the Roosevelt family in memory of Theodore Roosevelt (founder and first president of the Boone and Crockett Club), and his sons, Theodore Roosevelt, Jr., and Kermit Roosevelt.*

It is presented as an exemplar symbol of the Boone and Crockett Club's principles of conservation, fair chase hunting ethics and records keeping. Since its creation in 1948, this highest award has been bestowed upon only 17 fortunate hunters, in recognition of an outstanding North American Big Game "trophy worthy of great distinction" taken by them. For the most part, this honor has been assigned for mature animals with the highest scoring antlers, horns, or skull of a given species recorded under the B&C measurement system and rules of fair chase at the time of the award.

YEAR	HUNTER	CATEGORY	SCORE	PAGE
1948	Robert C. Reeve	Alaska Brown Bear	29-13/16	43
1949	E.C. Haase	Rocky Mountain Goat	56-6/8	46
1950	Dr. R.C. Bentzen	Wapiti	441-6/8	48
1951	George Lesser	Woodland Caribou	405-4/8	50
1953	Edison Pillmore	Mule Deer	203-7/8	53
1957	Frank Cook	Dall's Sheep	185-6/8	21
1959	Fred C. Mercer	Wapiti	419-4/8	55
1961	Harry L. Swank Jr.	Dall's Sheep	189-6/8	35
1963	Norman Blank	Stone's Sheep	190-6/8	57
1965	Melvin J. Johnson	Whitetail	204-4/8	59
1973	Doug Burris Jr.	Mule Deer	226-4/8	61
1976	Garry Beaubien	Mountain Caribou	452	65
1986	Michael J. O'Haco, Jr.	Pronghorn	93-4/8	69
1989	Gene C. Alford	Cougar	16-3/16	103
1992	Charles E. Erickson Jr.	Coues' Whitetail	155	73
2001	Gernot Wober	Rocky Mountain Goat	56-6/8	79
2010	Paul T. Deuling	Mountain Caribou	459-3/8	117

However, this select group possesses even more momentous situations when one goes beyond the exceptional trophy and takes into account the hunters and their unique stories. Among these are the two top-ranking Dall's sheep taken by Sagamore Hill Award winners Frank Cook and Harry L. Swank, Jr. The No. 2-ranking ram was taken by Cook in 1956. At the time of his Sagamore Hill Award in 1957, his trophy ranked No. 1. Swank's ram, taken and awarded the honor in 1961, has stood as No. 1 since that time.

Wild sheep and a relatively few other creatures survive and thrive in occasionally gravity-defying and inconceivably gorgeous wild places. For all lovers of the outdoors, these are the places the dreamers want to be, and the doers actually take on, come what may. As such, larger-than-life stories are more likely to emanate from this world. And in these unique hunter's stories—and in the other select Sagamore Hill Medal winner's stories elsewhere in this book—readers can find hopes, patience, planning, effort, pursuit, and the place where circumstances collide at the intersection of life events, dreams, and statistical improbabilities. Such is (or can be) life.

Epic Accounts of the Top Two Dall's Sheep

It is notable that of the top-50, top-25, and top-10 Dall's and Stone's sheep qualifying and recorded in the Boone and Crockett Club's records, only a comparatively few have been taken by hunters since 1970, let alone since the year 2000. This is shown (see table opposite) in sharp contrast to the number of exceptional bighorn and desert sheep taken in these more recent periods. For example, since 1970, almost 80 percent of the top-50 bighorn sheep, and just over two-thirds of the highest-scoring desert sheep have been harvested. The same analysis reveals that only 16 percent of the top-50 Dall's and Stone's sheep have been taken and added to the records over the last 34 years. This factor alone makes the top Dall's and Stone's sheep that much more unique and important from a historical perspective. It also raises questions as to the determinants contributing to these distinct differences in statistical trends.

One could surmise from the records data that bighorn and desert sheep populations have long outnumbered those of the Dall's and Stone's sheep—at least in terms of huntable numbers of the species. Further, and again overly simplistically, it would at least appear that bighorn and desert rams have experienced comparatively improving habitat and living conditions (i.e. the ability to attain old age and large horns) since 1970 versus Dall's and Stone's sheep. Whether or not these factors are relevant in terms of B&C's records and the status of wild sheep populations, the observations as to the top-trophy rankings is nonetheless very intriguing.

In all likelihood, a wide array of determinants, including the suppositions regarding relative species abundance and then-versus-now habitat and survival rates are involved. During the post-World War II years, for example, the increasing penetration of Alaska and the Canadian province's mountains and tundra by small, private aircraft very well had a direct bearing on the sheer number of Dall's and Stone's sheep accessible and taken by hunters. Given this relatively new mode of transportation, the added efficiencies (faster

Sheep Species	# of Top 50 Rams Since 1970	% of Top 50 Rams Since 1970	# of Top 50 Rams Since 2000	% of Top 50 Rams Since 2000
Dall's	8	16%	3	6%
Stone's	8	16%	4	8%
Bighorn	39	78%	24	48%
Desert	34	68%	11	22%

Sheep Species	# of Top 25 Rams Since 1970	% of Top 25 Rams Since 1970	# of Top 25 Rams Since 2000	% of Top 25 Rams Since 2000
Dall's	4	16%	1	4%
Stone's	3	12%	1	4%
Bighorn	23	79%	15	52%
Desert	18	67%	4	15%

Sheep Species	# of Top 10 Rams Since 1970	% of Top 10 Rams Since 1970	# of Top 10 Rams Since 2000	% of Top 10 Rams Since 2000
Dall's	1	10%	0	0%
Stone's	0	0%	0	0%
Bighorn	9	69%	6	46%
Desert	6	60%	1	10%

Data from B&C's On-Line Trophy Search.

travel and therefore fewer required hunting days) made selective hunting a far more viable option as well—adding specific pressure to the older age class rams. These factors, in turn, were strongly supported by a return to domestic economic prosperity during the 1950s and '60s.

The factors noted above do not consider many other positive or negative contributors. These could obviously include human population dynamics, habitat deterioration, industrial exploitation, impacts of regional game laws, numbers of licenses or tags sold, and other variables likely to affect the various sheep species' fortunes.

In any case, the Dall's and Stone's sheep appear to be the relative underdogs of the four North American wild sheep species today. This has not gone unnoticed by the Wild Sheep Foundation (WSF). In the July/August 2014 issue of *Sports Afield*, an interview with WSF's CEO and B&C Professional Member Gray N. Thornton included the following comments:

"The range of thinhorns (Dall's and Stone's sheep) is largely intact. There are challenged areas, though."

He went on to note that the organization recently held a Thinhorn Summit to devise an action plan for the two subspecies across their ranges in both Alaska and the Canadian provinces. As with their Lower 48 and Mexico sheep brethren, disease transmission from domestic sheep and goats is the biggest threat to sheep populations. In addition, and more specific to Dall's and Stone's sheep, it is believed that a lack of comprehensive management plans for sheep populations, as well as a need to better manage all-terrain vehicle access to remote areas, are key issues to be addressed on behalf of these great sheep.

The Swank and Cook rams, taken five years apart, obviously share much in common with other top-scoring Dall's sheep. These characteristics are primarily long horn curl (for example, of the top-50 scoring Dall's rams, the longer horn in almost all cases exceeds 45 inches), heavy horn base circumferences (generally greater than 15 inches), and above-average quarter circumferences as one moves

Measurements	Swank Ram		Cook Ram	
	Right Horn	Left Horn	Right Horn	Left Horn
Length of Horn	48-5/8	47-7/8	49-4/8	44-2/8
Circumference of Base	14-5/8	14-6/8	14	13-7/8
Circumference at First Quarter	13-5/8	13-6/8	13-2/8	13-2/8
Circumference at Second Quarter	11-6/8	11-7/8	12-1/8	12-2/8
Circumference at Third Quarter	6-5/8	6-7/8	6-6/8	7-3/8
Subtotals	95-2/8	95-1/8	95-5/8	91
Less Circumference Differences	5/8		7/8	
Final B&C Score	189-6/8		185-6/8	
Widest Spread (not part of score)	34-3/8		24-3/8	

Swank Dall's Ram   *Cook Dall's Ram*

around the horn. Horn length for these two rams is outstanding. In fact, the Cook ram's longer horn, at 49-4/8 inches actually exceeds the comparable measurement of 48-5/8 inches for Swank's ram. (See table above for additional details.) Only one other Dall's sheep, the No. 3 ram taken by Jonathan T. Summar, Jr., in the Alaska Range in 1965, possesses a single horn curl measurement exceeding 48 inches. Two other rams in the records have a longer horn that just makes the 48-inch mark.

Horn curl, also called the length of horn measurement on the scoring sheet, provides an interesting natural dilemma at times. This is true for the scoring of all North American wild sheep horns under the Boone and Crockett scoring methodology. Older bighorn rams in particular tend to naturally broom or damage horn tips during their lives (including battles with other rams vying for dominance). Missing horn cannot be measured, so it is lost to the wild—and to the final score.

Interestingly (and fortunately), this often-exhibited brooming, or broken horn asymmetry is not doubly penalized by the Boone and Crockett's scoring system. This is notable, as side-to-side symmetry is a significant component of the overall B&C methodology. In the case of sheep, horn curl length is equal to "all that is there." In other words, there is no additional scoring penalty for the difference between a 45-inch horn on one side, and a 42-inch broomed horn on the other side. The score credit for this example is simply 87 inches, rather than 84 inches if the difference between the two were subtracted in the final scoring calculation.

The latter scoring credit, or 84 inches from the example above, is not the case for differences in horn length for the remaining horned big-game species. For example, if a Rocky Mountain goat's horns are naturally symmetrical, great, but if one is shorter than the other, or broken off, the difference between the two horns is subtracted from the final score. That is because it wasn't grown (shorter) or is missing (broken). Sheep are therefore given the benefit of the doubt that horn length is likely asymmetrical in direct relation to the tendency for broomed horns, especially in mature bighorn and desert rams.

Therefore, B&C captures the bulk of the visual symmetry—or balance—for exceptional sheep in its circumference measurements. For the Swank and Cook rams, deductions of only 5/8 and 7/8 inches, respectively, were taken for circumference asymmetry. As with broomed or broken-horn tips, circumference measurements may be thrown askew when chunks of horn are missing, often as a result of fighting. Specifically, no score credit can be given for missing horn sections at the points at which circumference measurements are taken.

Taking this measurement observation to an extreme (specifically for Dall's and Stone's sheep), we compare the top-ranking rams with a hypothetically perfectly symmetrical ram scoring 180 inches, which would place it in the top-23 rams in the B&C All-time records as of this writing. Assuming 45-inch horn lengths, half of the total score would be from horn length, and the other half from circumference measurements.

Horn length and mass are certainly key wow-factor elements when comparing sheep horns, especially when viewed side-by-side. This is particularly true when looking at two otherwise full-curl rams, where one carries either heavier base circumferences and/or heavy mass all the way around the curl. However, a missing element that can also make outstanding rams' horns visually stunning is the widest spread of the horns, though this purely aesthetic characteristic is not factored into the overall scoring calculation.

The Boone and Crockett Official Measurers manual notes that sheep horn conformation may be any of three basic types: the close curl, a close curl with flaring tips, or wide-flaring horns. Thinhorn sheep, like the Dall's and Stone's species, tend to exhibit less brooming and damage than their bighorn or desert sheep counterparts. Conversely, they tend to display more variation in conformation and flare, which in turn decreases or increases outside spread. Greatest spread and tip-to-tip spread, while recorded on the official B&C score sheet, are not added to final score. This is important, as the range of basic horn conformation would discriminate against rams with close curl and lack of tip flare versus those possessing flaring tips or wide-flaring horns.

Therefore, and of special note as it relates to the Swank and Cook rams, two trophy sheep with comparable horn length and strong circumference measurements can still look very different. This is based on the tightness of the horn curl and/or how the horn tips flare out to create a total, visual outside dimension. In this specific case, the Swank ram's widest spread is a full 10 inches greater than that of the Cook ram. The specific measurement for Swank's sheep is 34-3/8 inches, versus 24-3/8 inches for Cook's.

Following are the two stories written by the hunters of these two incredible Dall's sheep.

Frank Cook

Finest Ever Taken

Frank Cook

Alaska Dall's Sheep | Current Rank #2

THE SHEEP WERE ON THE BARE STEEP SLOPE OF A MOUNTAIN FOUR or five miles away, and even through the binoculars they looked like no more than five small white specks.

"It's too late to get over there today," Frenchy Lamoreaux grunted, "and I'm not for siwashing in the open overnight unless we have to. I'm gonna move up ahead and have a look at that draw we saw from lower down. There might just be a ram in it."

CIRCA **1956**

"You go along," I agreed. I don't think any more of siwashing than you do, but I want to look those sheep over with the spotting scope before I pull out. Five together could be all rams, and there's always the chance of a good one in a bunch like that."

Frenchy moved off. I set up my 40x scope, stretched out prone behind it, and went to work on the far-off band of sheep. I was lying on a deep-cut sheep trail just below a 7,000-foot peak, and the weather that afternoon wasn't exactly mild. An icy wind poured over the ridge above me, howling like a banshee, and even on the low tripod that supported it, I couldn't hold the scope steady enough for a good, clear look.

So I rolled aside, scooped out a shallow depression in the rocky ground, set the tripod on it, and braced the scope with my packboard. That did it. I could get a good look at the five sheep now, and I studied them one by one.

The first three were just sheep—white blobs on the green-streaked, slate-gray slope. Though the scope was magnifying them 40 times, they were too far away for me to make out horns. Then something happened that made me suck in my breath. When I moved the scope to the fourth, I saw, clearly and distinctly even at that distance, the dark curl of horns.

I knew that I was looking at a Dall's head of far better than average size. I rested my eyes, then took another look to make sure the light and wind weren't playing tricks on me. The horns were still there, and when I rolled away from the scope my mind was made up. That ram was the kind I'd come for, and if he'd stick around I'd get him if it took me the rest of the season.

Frenchy came back within an hour and we headed for camp. Weather permitting, we agreed, we'd make our try the next morning. We'd get an early start, for this was going to be no easy mission.

The time was late August, 1956. Frenchy, Wally Wellenstein, and I were camped in the Chugach Mountains, north of Anchorage, Alaska. We were after one thing and one only, Dall's sheep, and we wanted good heads or none. We'd already had enough action and excitement to make the hunt stack up as a worthwhile venture. Now it seemed likely we were getting close to the climax.

I've enjoyed hunting since I was old enough to lug a gun, and Alaska has been in my blood as far back as I can remember. I grew up in New York, and there's some nice outdoors there, but the idea of one sprawling mountain range big enough to cover that whole state always appealed to me. So it was only natural, when I finished at the University of Denver after a hitch in the Navy, that I should head for Alaska. My work was to be that of tax consultant and investment representative, but I saw no reason why I shouldn't combine my favorite pastime with it. I settled in Anchorage in 1951, and still live there with my wife and young son.

I hunted moose my first season in Alaska, dropping a good

Kenai Peninsula specimen with one shot from my .300 Magnum. Then I set my sights on Dall's sheep, the milk-white thinhorns of Alaska and Yukon heights. A Dall's ram is one of the world's finest trophies—and correspondingly hard to get.

My first few sheep hunts were disappointing, but they taught me a lot. I learned that my daily office routine was poor training for climbing jagged heights until the clouds were below me. Regular sessions of roadwork fixed that. I trained before each hunt until I could run two miles in 16 minutes and tote a 100-pound pack a mile without stopping.

In my years of apprenticeship, during which I killed three fair Dall's sheep, I learned to travel light, relying on dehydrated foods and a minimum of light, but sturdy gear. Experience taught me to allow at least 20 days for a backpacking sheep hunt. Sheep-country storms can keep you in camp for days. You need time to wait out the weather.

I gradually acquired the right kind of optical equipment—light 7x35 binoculars and two spotting scopes, 25x and 40x. The 25x is for those warm days when the more powerful 40x picks up heat waves that distort objects.

I spent a lot of time planning for my 1956 hunt. This was to be the hunt for an outstanding trophy. If I couldn't locate a real buster I'd hold my fire.

After many talks with hunters, hikers, pilots, and prospectors, I settled on the Chugach Mountains as the place most likely to give me the kind of head I was looking for. I'd first hunted there in the fall of 1955 with Red Mayo, a former Maine guide. Sweating under heavy packs, Red and I had spent three days climbing up to that sheep range. That was too much.

I couldn't bear to think of walking in there again, so when I was ready for my hunt the next fall I decided to fly in to a small mountain meadow that was within easy walking distance of what I knew to be top-notch sheep range.

Red couldn't go, so I talked Wally Wellenstein into taking a week off to hunt with me. I felt a little guilty about it, for I wondered how we would salvage his job with an Anchorage architect firm if we stayed the whole 20 days I had in mind. But Wally didn't seem worried. He's lived Alaska since 1949, has spent most of his spare time hunting, and won second place in the 1953 Boone and Crockett Club competition with a polar bear.

Sheep season would open on Monday, August 20, so we made a date with Jack Lee, a local guide and pilot, to fly us to our base camp site the preceding Saturday. This would give us a couple of days to get camp established and scan the country for sheep. It was a beautiful morning for our flight, and as we bounced along through the rough air currents, we picked out bands of sheep on the green slopes and high meadows below. Jack set us down on our chosen airstrip, and after we'd unloaded our gear he took off into the morning sky and headed back to Anchorage. So far as we could see we had the whole Chugach Range to ourselves.

We spent the first day near the meadow where we'd landed. I'd hunted there the fall before and sheep were plentiful, but a year's time had brought changes. It was quickly apparent that I wasn't going to be able to keep the rosy promises I'd made Wally about good rams right around the airstrip. We saw four ewes and lambs that forenoon, and after lunch we checked a steep box canyon and spotted two rams, one three-quarter curl and one full curl, on the slides above us. Even the bigger one wasn't an outstanding head, and anyway, it would have taken rope and pitons to get up to him. We wrote him off, and agreed our best bet would be to move camp to another area higher up.

We made the climb Sunday, lugging gear and supplies over glaciers and steep slides, detouring around vertical cliffs we couldn't climb, wading ice-cold streams milky with glacial silt, and stopping frequently to rest and glass the mountains.

We saw nothing outstanding, and late in the afternoon we halted and made camp at the edge of a big snowfield just below the summit of a mountain. It was a bleak, wind-swept spot, but it had strategic value for us since it overlooked a long, beautiful valley, half a dozen hanging glaciers, and a tumbled range of cliffs and slides that looked ideal for sheep. And by climbing 200 yards to the top we could glass a vast area on the far slope.

We spent an hour or two glassing the country, and counted 23 sheep and 19 goats. Somewhat to our surprise, the goats were grazing lower down than the sheep. We were high enough to get at almost any band we chose, and we felt good about our prospects. "Looks as if we came to the right place," Wally said.

The weather turned dirty as evening came on with fog, rain, and sleet. We rigged a windbreak of our packboards and sheet of plastic, cooked supper in the lee of it, and at 7 o'clock, long before dark, we crawled into our sleeping bags to keep warm. We were ready for bed anyway—it had been a hard day.

I crawled out at 5 o'clock the next morning and broke an inch of ice on the water bucket. Breakfast consisted of side pork, stew and noodles reheated from the previous evening, bread and butter, and strong hot coffee. We figured we needed a meal that would stick to our ribs, for sheep season was open now and big doings were afoot.

We decided to try the far slope, across the glacier, where we'd sighted two good size rams—one conspicuously bigger than the other—the afternoon before. It was Wally's first sheep hunt and he was pretty keyed up.

We crossed the glacier in the early dawn as ribbons of fog rolled up out of the valley like gray smoke. On the far side we stopped to do some glassing, and within five minutes picked out our two sheep feeding on an open slope a couple of miles away, about where we'd seen them the previous day. We felt they'd probably hang around and wait for us if we didn't spook them.

The stalk promised to be a tough one. The wind was in our favor, but there was little cover and no way to approach out of sight of the rams, either below or above them. We worked along as carefully as we could, taking advantage of draws and ravines to make brief rests. The last 1,000 yards we moved over slowly, inching along when the rams turned their backs or lowered their heads to feed, halting whenever they looked our way. By now we could see that the bigger of the pair had remarkable horns.

Four hours from the time we left camp we were close enough for a shot. The earlier overcast weather had broken, and shooting light was perfect as we crawled to the top of a low hummock 130 yards below the nearest sheep. The bigger ram was high on the crown of the slope, while his smaller companion grazed nearby in a small hollow. The situation couldn't have been better for us, since the lower sheep was out of sight, except for the top of his back, and there was no danger of spooking him.

Since I'd given the shot to Wally (because it was his first chance at a sheep), I readied my camera and dropped back a few yards, looking for a good vantage spot. But in that instant, while Wally's head and shoulders were in sight over the hummock and I was creeping across an exposed slope, the ram threw up his head and saw us.

I froze in my tracks, still as a rock, and I think Wally held his breath. But it did no good—you can't out freeze or outstare a Dall's sheep. I lay on the steep slope in an awkward, cramped position, knowing it would be only a matter of minutes before I'd have to move. It was a question now of whether Wally could get off his shot before the ram figured us out and lammed.

Seconds dragged by while Wally slid his .30-06 Mannlicher up over a flat rock in front of him. I was holding my breath now. The ram was facing him head-on, and the curve of the slope hid all of the big white body except a patch of shoulder and the neck. I knew Wally wouldn't risk a head shot, not on such a trophy as that. *Would he miss altogether?*

Then, while I waited for the slam of the rifle, the ram took things into his own hands. He wheeled and raced for a jumble of rock to his left, and the gun barked out its hard, whiplash report.

The heavy bullet, centered squarely in the shoulder, should have knocked the ram off his feet. But it didn't. He swung uphill, running as if he hadn't been hit at all. Then the second shot missed a vital area but turned him back downslope, and the third dumped him in his tracks.

The head was a good one—in fact we didn't realize just how good at the time. We admired the horns, thumped each other on the back, made a few pictures, and went at the job of caping and skinning, boning out the meat and protecting it in a cotton sack for the trip back to camp. It made a heavy load, but we were too excited to mind.

We were back on the glacier, within a mile of camp, when dense fog rolled across the ice without warning, and in half a minute we were socked in. I've always carried a compass on my sheep hunts, but it was of no use now, for the fog had come so swiftly I'd had no time to take a bearing. We could see neither sky nor landmarks, only the ice for a few feet around us, and no man in his right senses goes wandering around on a glacier under those conditions. There's too great a chance of winding up at the bottom of a crevasse. So Wally and I slipped off our packs and sat down. An hour later the fog lifted as swiftly as it had come. It could have been worse, for we might have had to spend the night on the open glacier.

We were almost back to camp, just before dusk, when we saw a magnificent ram on a mountain less than a mile away, and for a few minutes I thought I had my trophy. Through the 40x spotting scope I could see massive horns—the best I'd ever laid eyes on. But while we were making excited plans to go after him the first thing in the morning, he swung his head and gave us a look at his left horn. It was splintered back for more than six inches, and the instant I saw it I lost all interest. My guess is he's as good as one-horned by this time, for if a challenger socked into him hard and solid during the rut last fall, that splintered horn is probably broken off.

I spent the next two days checking valleys, peaks, and canyons. I saw some fair sheep, but none I was willing to settle for. Wally, meanwhile, was making shuttle trips back to the airstrip with his trophy and part of the camp gear. Jack Lee had agreed to fly in each Saturday and check with us, and we decided it would be best for Wally to send his sheep back to Anchorage as soon as possible.

I helped Wally with the last leg of the shuttle late the second afternoon. As we set up camp at the airstrip shortly before dark, we found we had a neighbor, Frenchy Lamoreaux, an Anchorage guide who'd come in to scout the area for sheep and take a few pictures. Since Wally had his ram, Frenchy and I decided to team up for the rest of our stay, and I was to plan the hunt. We didn't think it would be as short as it was.

We started seeing scattered bands of sheep right after we left camp next morning, but we encountered nothing of trophy size until late afternoon. Then, on a mountain far ahead, we spotted the five rams I mentioned in the beginning, one of which had an unusually large head. I felt confident, as we crawled into our bags that night, that the climax of my sheep-hunting experience was only a few hours away. I was up and lighting the stove for breakfast at 3 o'clock. We bolted a hearty breakfast, then loaded up and walked away from camp in the first gray light of a cold, rainy morning.

We traveled steadily for hours in the rain and biting wind, climbing in and out of canyons, skirting slides too steep to cross. The route we had picked led up through a high pass to the slope where we'd seen the five sheep the afternoon before. We crossed the summit in a roaring storm, with rain blowing up one side of the mountain and snow up the other. If our five rams hadn't moved, we were getting close now, but an impassable snow ridge blocked the way above the pass. We'd have to drop down a shale slide and come up to the sheep from below.

We started down, skidding and loosening small avalanches of shale, but before we'd gone far we saw a band of 20 ewes and lambs on a slope at the bottom of the slide. To spook them into the five rams, assuming the latter were still in the neighborhood, would end our hunt, so we turned around and clawed our way back up the slide to look for another approach.

We found a well-worn sheep trail angling up toward the pasture where we hoped to make contact, but as we turned to follow it, two young rams came over the skyline above and marched down toward us. We were boxed in, with the big band below and this pair above. If any of them winded or saw us, the odds were good we could say good-bye to the five we were after. Reluctantly we turned off the sheep trail, climbing on steep, wet, slippery shale, and managed to get out of sight of the two that were coming down.

The rest of the way was almost straight up, and it was half an hour before we finally broke over the ridge—winded, rain-soaked, and tired. But it was worth the climb. The sheep pasture I'd studied through the spotting scope the afternoon before lay spread out in front of us now, a perfect haven for an isolated band of big rams. It was cut off from above by glaciers and snow, from below by rock walls too sheer to climb, and from the sides by shale slides and steep ravines. So far as we could see, we'd gained entrance over about the only possible route.

The sheep trail we'd started to follow came up the bottom of a ravine only a short distance below us. We dropped down and followed it out onto the open slope. Our five rams were nowhere in sight; but if they hadn't left the pasture, we had to be very close. Another 10 minutes would tell the story. I could feel my heart thumping against my ribs, and I knew it wasn't altitude alone that was doing it.

We were picking our way along, making no more commotion than two cats on a velvet rug, when suddenly we walked smack into a flock of ptarmigan. We had no warning. They materialized out of the hazy background of fog and rain, and perched on rocks on both sides of us. I held my breath, waiting for the usual cackle of alarm, knowing it might be all the warning the rams would need if they were close by. But not a bird called. Maybe the weather was too much for them, for they sat glum and silent, feathers fluffed out to fend off the cold rain, while we walked carefully on.

A little farther along a gray marmot streaked past us, racing for his den under a flat rock, and again I waited for the shrill alarm whistle that's standard marmot procedure in such cases. But the marmot ducked into his hole without a sound, and we heaved a sigh of relief and went on.

I was a few steps ahead of Frenchy, and I walked onto the five rams the way you'd walk up on tame sheep in a pasture. I rounded a big rock and there they were, 100 yards below, standing shoulder-to-shoulder and looking straight at us. It was one of the most breathtaking sights I've seen in a lifetime of hunting.

I ducked back and stopped Frenchy, but not before the sheep had caught motion. They weren't spooked but they were thoroughly alerted, and it wasn't likely they'd hang around very long. We swung to the left, up a rocky outcrop to get into shooting position, and the instant we looked over we knew we had them flat-footed. To their left was a deep ravine that would shelter them for 150 yards, but they'd still be within range when it petered out, with another 100 yards of bare meadow to travel. If they went to the right they had about the same distance of open slope to cross. Whichever way they chose, we'd have clear shooting.

The seconds ticked off while we tried to pick the two we wanted out of the tight-bunched group. They were all good heads, but at the back of the band shielded by the rest, I spotted what I was looking for—a massive set of horns that would go a lot better than full curl.

The two rams farthest downhill broke first. They wheeled and went for the ravine, and I realized it was time to shoot. But the other three still waited, as if not quite certain where the danger lay or which way to run. The one I wanted was hidden behind his two companions, as I held the scope on all three and waited. Then the two out in front spun around and lit out after the first pair, and as they broke apart I got the chance I wanted.

The big fellow hesitated long enough for me to center my crosshairs on his shoulder, and the 130-grain Silvertip from my .270 King Sporter knocked him over as if mountain lightning had struck. But he didn't stay down. He rolled a few yards down the slope, gathered his legs under him, and staggered to his feet. I hammered in another shot and he dropped.

Frenchy's .30-06 bellowed twice at my elbow, but the ram he'd picked kept going across the open slope beyond the ravine, and I saw the range was pretty long for iron sights. I shoved my rifle at him. "Try this," I said. "You can find him with the scope."

He dropped his gun, grabbed mine and brought it up, but nothing happened. "It won't shoot," he howled, and I realized I'd flipped the safety on automatically after my second shot. I reached across and thumbed it off. The ram had only about 20 yards to go now to get out of sight, and was pouring on coal. I didn't think Frenchy was going to make it, but at the bark of the .270 the sheep nose-dived into the shale and rolled end-over-end.

When I looked back at my own ram he wasn't as dead as I'd thought. He was up on his forelegs, dragging himself down the slope. I yanked my rifle away from Frenchy and put a third shot into his spine, and he was mine for keeps.

The slope where he died was so steep we couldn't cape him out there, so we dug a shallow trench across the shale and dragged him to a narrow shelf. When we put the tape on him it showed his right horn to be 49-1/2 inches long, the longest ever recorded on a Dall's sheep. My heart skipped a couple of beats. This could be a new world record head.

We caped the two sheep, loaded our packboards, and headed for camp. The horns of my ram, I learned later, weighed 27 pounds, and with my gun and other paraphernalia I was carrying close to 70 pounds. It was a long hard trip across the shale, off that mountain and up another to camp, and when we finally plodded in shortly before dark, we had a tough 16-hour day behind us. But I can't recall a day that ever paid more handsome dividends.

Wally had a steaming-hot supper ready for us, but when we showed our trophies, everybody forgot about eating for a few minutes. After a short meeting of the mutual admiration society, we sat down and licked our plates clean.

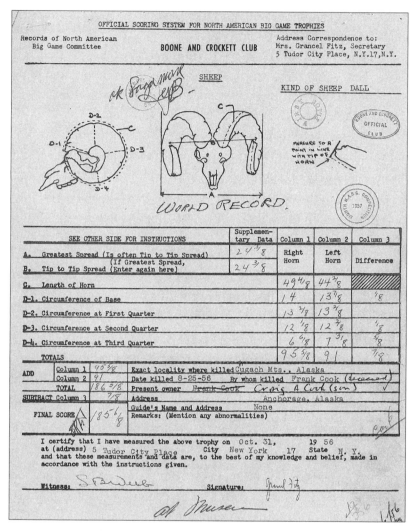

OFFICIAL SCORING SYSTEM FOR NORTH AMERICAN BIG GAME TROPHIES

Records of North American
Big Game Committee

BOONE AND CROCKETT CLUB

Address Correspondence to:
Mrs. Grancel Fitz, Secretary
5 Tudor City Place, N.Y.17,N.Y.

SHEEP

KIND OF SHEEP DALL

WORLD RECORD.

SEE OTHER SIDE FOR INSTRUCTIONS	Supplemen-tary Data	Column 1	Column 2	Column 3
A. Greatest Spread (Is often Tip to Tip Spread)	24 3/8	Right Horn	Left Horn	Difference
(If Greatest Spread, **B.** Tip to Tip Spread (Enter again here)	24 3/8			
C. Length of Horn		49 4/8	44 2/8	
D-1. Circumference of Base		14	13 7/8	1/8
D-2. Circumference at First Quarter		13 2/8	13 3/8	
D-3. Circumference at Second Quarter		12 1/8	12 2/8	1/8
D-4. Circumference at Third Quarter		6 4/8	7 3/8	5/8
TOTALS		95 5/8	91	7/8

ADD	Column 1	95 5/8	Exact locality where killed Cugach Mts., Alaska
	Column 2	91	Date killed 8-25-56 By whom killed Frank Cook (deceased)
	TOTAL	186 5/8	Present owner Frank Cook Craig A Cook (son)
SUBTRACT Column 3		7/8	Address Anchorage, Alaska
FINAL SCORE	185 6/8		Guide's Name and Address None
			Remarks: (Mention any abnormalities)

I certify that I have measured the above trophy on Oct. 31,   19 56
at (address) 5 Tudor City Place   City New York   17 State N. Y.
and that these measurements and data are, to the best of my knowledge and belief, made in
accordance with the instructions given.

Witness: **Signature:**

Next day the three of us hiked back for the meat. It was on that trip that we witnessed one of the rarest sights I'd ever seen, a battle between a three-quarter curl ram and a bald eagle. The eagle came close to winning, too. The ram had crossed a ridge above us and started over a shale slide where no man would have dared to venture. The eagle appeared out of nowhere and dived on him like a jet. The sheep all but lost his footing on the slippery shale, a fall which would have meant certain death, but he recovered and ducked for shelter under a nearby ledge with incredible speed and agility. He rested there while the eagle circled overhead.

Finally the sheep made a dash across the slope for the safety of a ravine. The eagle swooped down on him a couple of times, but couldn't get at him. This encounter proved something I'd long suspected, that eagles do sometimes prey on sheep, even full-grown ones.

The weather cleared and Jack Lee flew in to return us to Anchorage on August 25. We hurried to get our heads measured by experts. I was especially eager, for I knew I had a very unusual ram.

It turned out that all three of us had killed record-class Dall's rams. Entered in Boone and Crockett Club competition, Wally's scored 163-6/8 points, very good for a first sheep, as he remarked with a satisfied grin. Frenchy's went a little better, with 164-4/8 points, and I had done better still.

When Harry Swank and Capt. Louis Yearout, official Boone and Crockett measurers, taped my trophy they indicated a firm belief that I'd taken a new world-record sheep. But that still didn't make it official. I shipped the horns to B&C headquarters in New York, and the days dragged by while I chewed my nails and waited for the final word. Finally, on October 25, two months to the day after we got home, a wire from Mrs. Grancel Fitz, the record committee's secretary: "Congratulations on your new world's record Dall's sheep."

I guess I was the happiest hunter on earth, and a lot of other Alaska sportsmen were pleased too. I'd taken the best white sheep head ever collected, and Alaska had finally copped top honors from the Yukon Territory. The previous record, which had stood since 1948, was a ram that scored 182-2/8 killed near Champagne by Dr. Earl J. Thee.

Our hunt had proved what I'd believed for two or three years, that the biggest Dall's ram alive would be found in the remote, high pastures of the Chugach Range. Is there another up there even bigger? Only time will tell, but I mean to go back and have a look every now and then.

Story originally appeared in the October 1957 issue of OUTDOOR LIFE.
Reprinted with permission of Craig Cook, Frank's son and current owner of the ram.

World's Record Dall's Sheep

Harry L. Swank, Jr.

Alaska Dall's Sheep | Current Rank #1

AS I SNUGGED THE .264 AGAINST MY SHOULDER, THE GREAT DALL'S ram moved closer to the edge of the ridge and peered down curiously. Instinctively I brought the crosshairs to bear, but as my finger tightened on the trigger doubts began to assail me. *Should I shoot or wait—try to get a closer look at the sheep?* He was a magnificent animal, but did he carry the world-record head that I'd been seeking for seven years?

CIRCA *1961*

A man must want a trophy pretty badly to put in all that time, and that man was me. So last season I went into the wild Wrangell Mountains of Alaska with my hunting partner, Perley Jones, and guide, Jack Wilson. From Jack's base camp at Gulkana we made a number of reconnaissance flights deep into the mountains and finally picked an area far back—one so shockingly rough and remote that it is seldom, if ever, visited by hunters. Then as August faded into September, Jack set us down on a big, tilted glacier, an operation that called for infinite skill. The country was as hostile as any a man is likely to meet: forbidding glaciers bounded by treacherous crevasses and moraines; cliffs whose sheer faces seemed insurmountable; miserable weather.

"After a good night's sleep, Perley and I made a blood-curdling, neck-risking descent down the side of the main glacier into the valley of a lesser one. Moving slowly up the canyon we carefully glassed the surrounding ridges. There were sheep, but nothing that looked like a world record. However, Perley found one to his liking and started a laborious climb up the canyon wall, while I set up our ultralight tent and made camp. Hours later he returned, disappointed: a wolverine had spooked his trophy just as he got within range.

By now it was well into the afternoon, but I decided to have a look at what lay beyond the next hill. The hill proved to be farther away than I'd estimated and the sun was getting dangerously low when I finally glassed the valley beyond it. Seeing nothing, I was about to return to camp when two rams appeared suddenly on a ridge a quarter mile away. One was only a youngster but the other was huge—bigger than any sheep I'd ever seen.

Caught out in the open, there was nothing I could do but try to get closer to the ram, and strangely enough I managed to get within 350 yards of it before the young sheep noticed me and started to act nervous. Groaning inwardly, I dropped to the ground and brought my rifle to bear on the big fellow. But then I hesitated. I wasn't at all sure he was of world-record stature, and if I shot him my hunt would be over for the year. Maybe—

Wham! The rifle went off almost by itself, before I'd made up my mind. The big ram leaped convulsively, then slumped to the ground. By now it was almost dark. Just time enough to dress the ram and hurry to camp.

Not until next morning did I know my seven-year quest was over. Carefully I measured the curl-and-a-third horns. The head was a new world's record! Later on the Boone and Crockett Club officially awarded it 189-6/8 points.

Did I say my quest was over? Well I'm not so sure. Someone is almost sure to get the next word-record Dall's, and it might as well be me!

Harry Swank's untimely end came in December 1963 when his plane crashed as he was taking his final solo flight for his twin-engine license. The trophy hunting world lost a friend.

Anchorage Daily Times
Monday - Sept. 11, 1961

RECORD DALL SHEEP BAGGED

A huge Dall sheep, unofficially measured at larger than the world's record, was bagged by Harry Swank Jr., local sportsman and operator of Van's Sporting Goods. The sheep's unofficial preliminary measurements totaled 192⅝ points by Boone and Crockett Club hunting standards. That is more than seven points larger than Anchorage tax consultant Frank Cook's present world record. Swank's sheep was taken in the Wrangell Mountains. Swank hunted with Perley Jones of the U.S. Army Engineer District, Alaska, and Jack E. Wilson of Wilson's Flying Service, Gulkana.

More Short Stories About Sagamore Hill Award Winners

Hanspeter Giger

SAGAMORE HILL AWARD-WINNING TROPHIES ARE BROADLY represented throughout this book. After all, the award was originally given for the highest-scoring antlers, horns, or skull of a given species recorded under the Boone and Crockett Club's measurement system and rules of fair chase at the time of the award; by definition, representative of the foundational elements of this book's stories.

The formulation and codification of the current version of the B&C big game scoring system came together in the middle of the 20th century, adopted in 1950, with the first publication based on (and outlining) the new methodology being the 1952 edition of *Records of North American Big Game*. The previously titled Big Game Competitions (now called Big Game Awards Programs) initiated in 1947 and held annually, began using the current version of the official measurement system starting in 1950.

This timeframe clearly overlapped with the development and initiation of the Sagamore Hill Award by the Roosevelt family. Notably, awards for the 1948 and 1949 competitions were made

Fred Mercer with his award-winning American elk. The bull—taken in 1958—scores 419-4/8 points. His story is featured on page 55.

before the current scoring system was adopted. They were awarded based on the selection by a Judges Panel. So, prior to that time, the Club's records-keeping efforts were largely represented by the National Collection of Heads and Horns and earlier scoring systems. The first scoring systems, initially developed starting in 1902, were comparatively primitive and uncomplicated but formed the basis used in compiling the first two editions (published in 1932 and 1939, respectively) of *Records of North American Big Game.*

In essence, early award-winning trophies were being added to the records at something we'll refer to here as a second inflection point in time for the Club's work. The first inflection point, some 50 years earlier, had resulted in the creation and inception of the Boone and Crockett Club at a time when the ultimate extinction of our native big game and many other species was considered a frightening but viable possibility. President Theodore Roosevelt's calls to action, in conjunction with a number of his forward-thinking and highly-capable colleagues, set in motion the institution, its core principles, and the early policies which continue to drive and guide us today.

During this second inflection point, the Club began collecting and recording records of North American big-game trophies. In addition, the early fruits of the North American Model of Wildlife Conservation began to emerge. Many big game trophies taken in earlier times were still being discovered, measured and entered into the records at the same time that an increase in the number of more recently harvested record specimens began to take off.

The formerly listed R.C. Bentzen's typical American elk (1950 award, now listed as hunter unknown) and Edison Pillmore typical mule deer (1953 award) represent examples of such early Sagamore Hill Award winners—trophies presented predominantly on the merits of scores relative to other high-ranking trophies of their (and all the other) species listed in the B&C records. Not surprisingly, Sagamore Hill Medals tended to be given to the hunters of new World's Records. Unfortunately, stories of these early award-winning hunts were not necessarily recorded in great detail. Further, the hunt details were not as likely to have been as fully scrutinized in the same way, especially given the even higher ethical hunting standards emblematic of the Sagamore Hill Medals bestowed in later years.

Most award winners in those early competitions largely represented the single-most outstanding trophy presented at the event, and therefore, not selected based on as many beyond-the-score factors as they are today. Developments in transportation and technology, among other considerations, prompted an evolution in the concept of fair chase and ethical hunting practices. As a result, the number of new requirements listed on the entry affidavit and hunt information forms have increased substantially over time.

Over the last two decades. New fair chase rules based on changing hunting equipment, methods, and other factors have increased the criteria scrutinized when considering a specific trophy for an award nomination. Although new World's Record trophies are still likely to be considered potential award winners today, not all hunters of a new top-scoring trophy are likely to receive the award based on the merits of high score/high rank and fair chase alone. As articulated in the 12th edition of *Records of North American Big Game:*

> To be eligible for nomination, the trophy must either be a new World's Record or one that is close to it. In addition, the hunt that produced the trophy should be exemplary of those characteristics most highly valued by Roosevelt: fair chase, self-reliance, perseverance, intentional selective hunting, and mastery of challenges being some of those. After reviewing the hunt accounts of possible candidates, the Judges Panel may choose to nominate a particular trophy for the Sagamore Hill Award. The nomination is reviewed by the Big Game Records Committee Chair who may choose to make further investigations before recommending the award to the Club.

Supporting the results of these *evolved* considerations, only four Sagamore Hill Medals have been awarded over the past 24 years, even though many more new World's Record and top trophies have been added to the records books. In essence, a very high bar has been re-set, and as such it remains one worthy of the original goals of the Club.

Even though the stories behind the award winners were not all recorded well or were necessarily epic in the sense of all-in adventure, hardship, etc., they have nevertheless stood the test of time as truly outstanding representatives of their big game species. As a testament to their individual merits, all but three of the 17 Sagamore Hill Award winners remain to this day in the top five ranks for their species in the All-time records. The remaining three are the only exceptions to a top-10 or top-25 records book rank: the Mercer typical American elk—a top-10 trophy (ranked No. 9 at this printing); the Reeve Alaska brown bear (ranked 30th in a five-way tie); and the Pillmore typical mule deer (ranked 132nd in a seven-way tie at this printing). In the end, no one can deny that they are all truly representative of the best examples of their wild and free-roaming species!

Most of the 17 B&C award-winners to date have at least some recorded hunt story to them. Many of these are included in this book as standalone stories. The remaining stories are included within this chapter.

- Robert C. Reeve, Alaska Brown Bear (1948)
- E.C. Haase Rocky Mountain Goat (1949)
- R.C. Bentzen/hunter unknown, Wapiti (1950)
- George H. Lesser, Woodland Caribou (1951)
- Edison A. Pillmore, Mule Deer (1953)
- Fred C. Mercer, Wapiti (1959)
- Norman Blank, Stone's Sheep (1963)
- Melvin J. Johnson, Whitetail Deer (1965)
- Doug Burris Jr., Mule Deer (1973)

These nine Sagamore Hill Award winners, some of which

lack hunt details, are nevertheless enriched by the contents of the B&C Club's records files and other sources of hunter details. All have been included to some degree in the pages that follow.

1948 Sagamore Hill Medal – Robert C. Reeve
Alaska Brown Bear – 29-13/16

Details of Robert C. Reeve's 1948 Alaska brown bear hunt are quite thin, but fortunately, epic-quality bear statistics and one photo in particular lend weight to the merits of his outstanding trophy. Given Reeve's background and extensive accomplishments—including landing planes on glaciers (the book *Glacier Pilot*, by Beth Day, was based on his story)—one has to consider that the hunt itself may have paled in comparison to the man's day-to-day life adventures!

Reeve moved to Alaska in 1932 with no plane and no money. However, he had fairly extensive experience as an aircraft mechanic and pilot, and carved his niche in the world as a pioneering Alaska pilot. Between bush flights and gold mine supply runs, he logged some 2,000 glacier landings. After World War II, he founded and operated Reeve Aleutian Airways, an airmail, passenger, and freight delivery service to the Aleutian Islands. In all, he logged some 14,000 hours of flying time during his life.

In a correspondence with the Club, through Dr. Harold E. Anthony at the American Museum of Natural History in New York City, Reeve enthusiastically accepted the invitation to attend and receive recognition for his bear at the 1948 North American Big Game Competition. In addition, he requested that several of his hunting colleagues, including a major general and two lieutenant generals of the Air Force be included as guests, along with Reeve and his wife. Reeve later confirmed his four guests and sent along a check in the amount of $16 to cover their costs for attending the event. He also crated and shipped the bear's hide to be present at the competition's awards presentation.

From Reeve's letter dated January 3:

It is my desire to contribute as much as possible to the success of the 1948 Competition. The hide of my record bear, now tanned and made up with a full head, is without a doubt the finest specimen of brown bear that has ever been killed. It is perfectly furred and processed, and in spite of shrinkage in drying and tanning, is still 10 feet wide and 9 feet long. Should the committee feel that they would like to include this bear in the public exhibition, I should be pleased to ship this rug to New York to arrive before January 19th.

We also have 1600 feet of color film of our last hunt showing about 50 brownies, include the actual stalking and shooting of my large brownie, and several others. I am bringing them with me and will be available for such private showings to the Club Members as may be desired.

Letters from Samuel Webb, later chair of the Records Committee, are included in the Reeve bear's file in the B&C Records archives. In one, Webb wrote, very politely and "politically correctly" (especially for the times): "You will note that there is also a photographic competition but if you send in your movies of the bear hunt, may I suggest that you do not show the sequence of the bear actually being killed. Photos, before and after, are always extremely interesting but a lot of discussion results when hunters show the actual kill."

Although the Alaska Department of Fish & Game brown bear fact sheet notes that a large coastal male brown bear may weigh up to 1,500 pounds, Reeve claimed his bear weighed some 1,800 pounds. In an article from *The Seattle Times* dated January 29, 1949, we note the following excerpt: "The flyer-sportsman, head of the firm which delivers air mail to the Aleutians, said he shot the bear May 26 near

Cold Bay, at the tip of the Alaskan Peninsula, soon after the beast had emerged from hibernation—hungry and mean. Had it been shot near the end of its normal salmon-eating season, Reeve estimated it would have weighed about 2,200 pounds."

In addition, written below the photo of the hunter with the bear, Reeve noted the hide, lying on the ground, measured 12 feet, 4 inches wide, and 10 feet, 4 inches long. These measurements, plus the following details, and the type of rifle Reeve used, are noted in *The Seattle Times* article as well: "Shoulder height of Reeve's bear was 5 feet 4 inches, and it measured more than 12 feet standing erect. It was killed with a Model 96 Winchester."

Should the measurements above be reasonably accurate, this was indeed a giant. For the records book, however, there are very good reasons that hides and weights are not included. Hides can very easily be badly mis-measured or stretched at the kill site, or before/after tanning. Weights, especially those of very large animals in remote places, would be nearly impossible to measure accurately, let alone consistently.

We'll never know with certainty the actual live weight or dimensions of Reeve's bear. However, between his piloting and cargo experience, and the equipment he may have had at his disposal (most likely at the nearest aircraft facilities), his measurements could have some validity. In any event—a huge bear! With final skull measurements of 29-13/16, Reeve's brown bear (ranked in a five-way tie for 30th at this printing) is 15/16 of an inch smaller than the current World's Record score of 30-12/16 inches.

Reeve was not only the accomplished aviator and Sagamore Hill Medal winner, but he later became a Regular Member of the Boone and Crockett Club. He also donated his award-winning bear trophy to the American Museum of Natural History.

OFFICIAL MEASURER'S NOTE: Just plain large! As bear skulls are scored based on length and width measurements, top-ranking Alaska brown bears range up to 1-1/2 inches longer or just over 1-1/4 inches wider than Reeve's trophy.

1949 Sagamore Hill Medal – E.C. Haase
Rocky Mountain Goat – 56-6/8

In addition to an archival photo (shown at right) from the 1949 competition and awards display, we are fortunate to have the following recap of E.C. Haase's hunt from Grancel and Betty Fitz, written in the 1964 edition of *Records of North American Big Game*:

> The fates also smiled on E.C. Haase, for his world-record Mountain Goat was the first he encountered on his first morning of climbing with Allen Fletcher, his guide. Packing out from Smithers, B.C., on September 15, 1949, their camp was made in the Babine Mountains. The huge solitary billy was spotted at about three hundred yards in the usual precipitous country, but it disappeared before a shot could be fired. When they saw it again, a few minutes

later, the range had stretched to nearly four hundred yards, with no way to get closer. Mr. Haase, shooting prone with a .30-06, killed it with his third shot, and although it fell off the ledge and rolled down the mountain several hundred feet, it lodged in a snowbank with its horns undamaged.

The hunt location is listed in the records as the Babine Mountains, British Columbia, Canada. Other than these tidbits and a photo of the mount, there appears to be very little additional information available on Haase's Rocky Mountain goat, or Mr. Haase himself. That said, Mr. Haase's trophy is currently owned by the Boone and Crockett Club's National Collection of Heads and Horns. It remains tied for the No. 2 position at 56-6/8 B&C points in the All-time records for Rocky Mountain goat. Haase's goat shares that position with Gernot Wober and L. Michalchuk's 2001 Sagamore Hill Award-winning goat (see story on page 79).

OFFICIAL MEASURER'S NOTE: Rocky Mountain goat horns don't offer a tremendous range of measurement stats, but Mr. Haase's trophy demonstrates both great length (12 inches even on each side, whereas the single-longest horn measurement in Trophy Search is 12-4/8 inches) and circumference measurements (6-4/8 inches for Haase's goat versus the highest top measurement of 6-6/8 inches found in Trophy Search). Only this billy's tip-to-tip spread measurement is significantly less than the most extreme example in the records—9 inches for the Haase goat, and the widest recorded spread is 13-2/8 inches. However, spread does not factor into the overall score calculation for goats.

1950 Sagamore Hill Medal – Dr. R.C. Bentzen Wapiti – 441-6/8

The Sagamore Hill Award presented to Dr. R.C. Bentzen for a wapiti (American elk) in 1950 was later listed and properly classified as hunter unknown. In the chapter, "Some Stories Behind the Records," by Grancel Fitz and included in the 1958 edition of *Records of North American Big Game*, Fitz wrote:

> Not much is known about the record Wapiti except that it came from the Big Horn Mountains of Wyoming, as far back as 1890. Nobody knows who shot it. Discovered by Dr. Bentzen in a barn, and remounted with a new cape, it can still claim a comfortable margin of more than 27 score points over its closest modern rival. The natural winter ranges of the Wapiti herds have been settled up since this gigantic specimen was taken. As the Wyoming bulls now have less favorable forage in the crucial time when they begin to grow their new antlers, this one may stand for many more years.

Sadly the actual hunter's name and story are not known, but this magnificent trophy bull's antlers stand on their own and still rank in the No. 3 position in the All-time Boone and Crockett records for

Boone and Crockett Judges (left to right–James Bond, Ernst von Lenerke, Frank Schramm, Milford Baker, and Grancel Fitz) measure the Bentzen bull during B&C's 4th Competition, which was held at the American Museum of Natural History in New York.

typical American elk. It is the only picked-up trophy to have ever received the Sagamore Hill Medal. This exceptional trophy is owned by the Jackson Hole Museum.

OFFICIAL MEASURER'S NOTE: Folks viewing trophy bull elk (especially typicals) may say they all look the same. Yes, but… the longest single point on a bull can (per Trophy Search) range up to a whopping 30-7/8 inches, greatest circumference measurements to 14-4/8 inches, greatest spread up to 63-3/8 inches and longest main beam as much as 66-3/8 inches. From each individual bull to the next, conformation differences can create a wide range of total score outcomes based on the combination of these factors. In the case of this bull specifically, it is the second-highest scoring 8x7 (points on right antler and left antler, respectively) in the B&C records. Further, exceptional beam length and symmetry—61-6/8 inches (right) and 61-2/8 inches (left)—and a longest point of 26-6/8 inches lend to its high overall B&C score.

FRONT VIEW
WOODLAND CARIBOU
NEWFOUNDLAND
KILLED BY
GEO.H. LESSER
JOHNSTOWN.N.Y.
SEPT 22-1951

1951 Sagamore Hill Medal – George H. Lesser
Woodland Caribou – 405-4/8

George H. Lesser was a taxidermist based in Johnstown, New York. His business letterhead has a fine vintage vibe to it. The line at the bottom of the letterhead is quite classic—especially relatable for those hunters who have endured long turnaround times for their mounted trophies: *Special notice—do not send us any orders for which you are in a hurry.* Let's call that fair and full disclosure!

As for the hunt, Mr. Lesser indicated in a letter to Samuel Webb, dated October 19, 1951, "I returned last week from Newfoundland with the biggest woodland caribou head taken there in a good many years. The game wardens and guides, as well as others who saw this head up there pronounced it the largest they had ever saw [sic]. It has 45 points with massive antlers and double brow points which overlap and lock in the front."

Unfortunately, no other hunt details were relayed by George Lesser, except that he had two hunting companions who also took caribou on this trip. However, Lesser's Newfoundland outfitter's son, Gary L. Saunders, later wrote a book including a short story of the hunt. In *Rattles and Steadies, Memoirs of a Gander River Man,* we find the following:

> In 1951 our outfitting business received a boost when one of our hunters took a world-class woodland caribou. I had hired my cousin Orlendo (Lindo) Gillingham to guide George Lesser of Johnstown, New York during the latter part of September. On the twenty-second, returning to camp after hunting all day with no luck, they spotted a big stag crossing Robinson's Bog. The stag was running and far away, but Lesser wanted to try for a shot anyway. Lindo, knowing caribou habits and not sure how good a shot Lesser was, advised him to be ready when the animal stopped. The puzzled hunter kept the stag in his sights and, sure enough, it hove to and looked at them, presenting a good broadside target though at long range. And thanks to Lindo's knowledge, the caribou's curiosity, and Lesser's good shooting, they got him.

According to correspondence in the B&C files, Mr. Lesser relayed, "I have killed a good many head of big game, but this Caribou is my prize, and I am sure it will make a great attraction when mounted and on display." Lesser's son, Richard G. Lesser, added additional details in a letter to Jack Reneau in 1993, after his father's death. "Enclosed are some brochures about George H. Lesser's life as a taxidermist. He was unique in that he hunted in the U.S. and Canada all his life, and made two trips to Africa which were extremely productive in taking record game, or near-record."

Richard Lesser wrote about the adventures of "Woody," as the senior Lesser's caribou came to be known. In 1991, Richard and his daughter Sue gave the trophy to Mr. Harold Pelley (of Glenwood, Newfoundland), who has an interesting connection to the senior Lesser's hunt.

After his mother died, Richard Lesser and his family had begun the process of finding a permanent home for Woody, which had hung in the senior Lesser's taxidermy shop for years. Neither Richard's parents nor his own family had sufficient space to house Woody but, "…none of the family wanted to find it suddenly necessary to call the trash man when the estate had to be liquidated." They had written to the National Rifle Association in early 1992, offering the trophy to the Boone and Crockett Club for free. However, as fate would have it, no connection was made through that letter.

From Richard Lesser's letter: "Similar to Snoopy in the Peanuts cartoon strip, on a cold and dark and stormy night, January 24, 1992, Mr. Pelley decided to see if he could find out about the record woodland caribou taken by George H. Lesser on September 16, 1951 when Mr. Pelley was a young man. All his life he was haunted by this uncertainty." Pelley made contact with the Lesser family, and later took possession of Woody after an adventurous trip during the winter thaw of the Gulf of St. Lawrence. Per Richard Lesser, "Woody finally arrived back 'home' April 23, 1991—approximately forty years after he left."

OFFICIAL MEASURER'S NOTE: Amongst its subspecies, Lesser's caribou's key scoring strengths are its interlocking double shovels, or brow tines, which are not only large, but amazingly symmetrical as well. Specifically, the lengths of the brow tines are precisely 20-1/8 inches per antler, and the widths of these tines are 19-4/8 and 19-5/8 inches. From Trophy Search, these measurements have reached maximum lengths of up to 24-4/8 inches for brow tine length, and 22 inches for brow tine width. Lesser's bull also stands out as having among the highest number of points, 43, versus 47 for the record trophy with the most points (although the number of points alone is not factored into the scoring calculation).

1953 Sagamore Hill Medal – Edison Pillmore
Mule Deer – 203-7/8

Sadly, there is virtually no information related to Edison Pillmore's hunt for his then-record typical mule deer.

An article from the *Greeley Daily Tribune* (Greeley, Colorado), dated Friday March 26, 1954, indicates that Pillmore's trophy was taken in the Jackson County, Colorado, area in 1949. Mr. Pillmore died before entering the head. His widow later submitted it for the records.

However, as Granzel Fitz wrote in the 1958 edition of *Records of North American Big Game*, we have a glimpse into the evolution of the category in terms of the number of trophy typical mule deer submitted for entry into the records, especially early on:

> Our new Mule Deer lists offer a close parallel in that the Typical record-holder is a comparatively recent head, while the Non-Typical leader is another old trophy with an obscure background. The reason, of course, is that nobody used to think of records unless the rack of antlers carried an exceptional number of points. A lot of the finest old Non-typical heads were treasured and preserved, while many fine Typical racks have been lost. The world record Typical head in the 1952 book was an old-time trophy that still has a larger basic structure than any Mule Deer rack ever

measured, so we have reason to think that more new records in this case are likely to turn up.

That champion in the 1952 lists carried four big abnormal points which totaled 24-7/8 inches in length. The resulting penalty brought the score down to 200-3/8, and this made it vulnerable. In the 1953 North American Big Game Competition, the late Edison Pillmore's trophy, from Jackson County, Colorado, raised the standard to 203-7/8. Then, in the 1954-55 Competition, the present world record was established when Horace T. Fowler's specimen was scored at 208-6/8. It is unfortunate that no other information on this one could be obtained, beyond the report that Mr. Fowler shot it in the North Kaibab country of Arizona in 1938. The same show, by the way, brought in other heads scoring 203-4/8, 201, and 200-3/8, which meant that the 1952 record-holder would have fared no better than a fourth-place tie.

Many outstanding typical mule deer have been added to B&C's records since Mr. Pillmore's trophy was entered and honored. As a singular specimen, it has fared the least well of the Sagamore Hill Medal winners in terms of the All-time rankings. Today, Pillmore's trophy ranks 132nd in a seven-way tie at 203-7/8. That said, it is with reasonable certainty that no one would turn down an opportunity for a buck like this!

OFFICIAL MEASURER'S NOTE: Not surprisingly, this typical mule deer trophy possesses all of the characteristics of a top-scoring buck—including modest asymmetrical aspects common to most natural antlers. A gross typical score of 213-1/8 nets significantly lower (9-2/8 points total) due to 3-3/8 inches of non-typical "character" points, including an extra point on the end of the left main beam, making it look like an open-end wrench, and a sticker point off the G2 on the deer's right antler. Otherwise, modest deductions came from side-to-side main beam, G3 and G4

An unidentified man holds the two medals awarded to Edison Pillmore's
mule deer trophy from the 1953 Competition.

asymmetry. Matching 3-inch brow tines (G1s) and most circumference measurements
over 5 inches round out this fine buck's impressive antler frame.

1959 Sagamore Hill Medal – Fred C. Mercer
Wapiti – 419-4/8

Fred Mercer's bull elk, taken in Madison County, Montana, in 1958, still ranks No. 9 in the All-time records for typical American elk. The state of Montana lists some 125 bulls netting over the 375 All-time minimum entry score, and Mercer's is one of only five Montana bulls scoring over 400 inches.

The September-October 2012 issue of *Montana Outdoors* included the following comments about Mercer's elk.

In 1958, Fred Mercer was working on his uncle's dairy ranch just south of Twin Bridges, Montana. In late October, the two took a week off to hunt the upper

Ruby River country, just as they had every year since 1946. In an article for *Outdoor Life* in 1960, Mercer wrote that he'd had a hunch he would find the bull of his dreams in the Gravelly Range, which he described as the 'rough and roadless country north of camp.' One morning at first light he took his .270-caliber rifle and headed out solo, walking through a few inches of sugar-soft snow. Soon he came across the biggest set of bull tracks he had ever seen. After following the tracks a while, Mercer figured the herd was an hour or so ahead of him. The bull, which may have sensed the hunter, circled his cows around Mercer. The herd caught his scent and took off running. Mercer wouldn't let up, however. After trailing the herd for another 12 miles or so, he changed tactics. He decided to cut the elk off when they reached a ridge at the head of an open canyon. Upon reaching the ridge top, he slowly peeked over. Not 50 yards away was the biggest bull he'd ever seen in his life, contentedly grazing broadside. Mercer's 150-grain soft-point hit the bull in the neck right below the ears. He fired once more and the hunt was over. After dressing the bull out to cool, Mercer made his way back to camp, arriving several hours after dark. For years the Mercer bull was the number two typical elk in the world. Today it stands at number 9. It's still the best typical elk Montana has ever produced.

OFFICIAL MEASURER'S NOTE: The strengths of Mercer's bull's antlers include an impressive 53-inch inside spread. Main beams of 59-7/8 inches for the right antler, and 60-1/8 inches for the left, are tremendous and nearly perfectly symmetrical. Lastly, Mercer's trophy is the third largest "clean" (no non-typical points) 7x7-point frame bull in the B&C records.

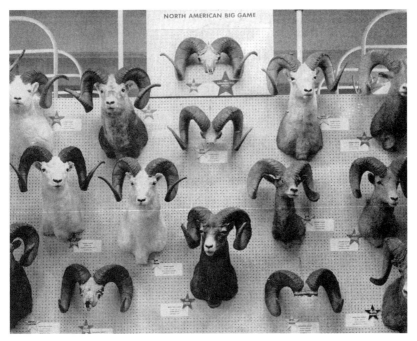

Blank's award-winning Stone's Sheep was featured at the top of the display for the 1963 Competition held at the Carnegie Museum in Pittsburgh, Pennsylvania.

1963 Sagamore Hill Medal – Norman Blank
Stone's Sheep – 190

As with the Dall's sheep, the Stone's sheep records also hold two exceptional top rams, notably those taken by L.S. Chadwick (Ranked No. 1) and Norman Blank (Ranked No. 2). These rams were harvested on the Muskwa and Sikanni Chief rivers of British Columbia, respectively. The hunt for Chadwick's ram occurred in 1936; Blank's in 1962. Blank was awarded the Sagamore Hill honor in 1963 for his outstanding ram. Had the Chadwick ram been taken two decades or so later, it may very well have become one of the first Sagamore Hill Medal winners. In a similar comparison to the Swank and Cook Dall's sheep, these exceptional rams have remained unchallenged for an extended period of time and may never be exceeded in the records books.

As many sheep hunters and studiers of big game records books know, the Chadwick Stone's sheep ram, taken in 1936 by L.S. Chadwick, is considered by many to be the most outstanding individual North American trophy animal of all time. In addition to its extreme horn length, mass, symmetry, and spread, it is the only ram of all four species of North American wild sheep that has 50-inch horn measurements on both sides. The longer left horn measures 51-5/8 inches. Amazingly, Norman Blank's No. 2 sheep's horns both measured exactly 46-6/8 inches. Although notably shorter overall than those of Chadwick's ram, they are superbly symmetrical. Also, with the exception of one circumference measurement (D4, or the third quarter measurement toward the horn tip) Blank's ram carries a bit more mass than the Chadwick ram.

From the 1964 edition of *Records of North American Big Game*, "Stories Behind the Records," by Grancel & Betty Fitz, we find the following entry:

> In 1962 Mr. Norman Blank, a young Californian, not too familiar with the Boone and Crockett Competitions, wrote as follows:

> 'I have just had the great good fortune to bag a Stone Sheep with a *field* score of 193. My guide, R. Lynn Ross of Pink Mountain, B.C., and I had a very fine hunt; it lasted most of one day after we spotted this big ram and it was killed at the head of Sikanni River, B.C.; it required the entire night to make our way off the mountain.

> 'We are pleased that our efforts were rewarded beyond any reasonable expectations, and I would like to know if this sheep is eligible for the next Big Game Competition?'

> Innocence is bliss! Mr. Blank sent his trophy in to the

1963 Exhibition and the official score was 190. This is the finest Stone ram reported since 1936, and it ranks #2 in the All-time records. This outstanding trophy won the highest of all awards, the Sagamore Hill Medal, and we are sure that Mr. Blank's expression, 'our efforts were rewarded beyond any reasonable expectations,' has been repeated many times!

1965 Sagamore Hill Medal – Melvin J. Johnson
Whitetail – 204-4/8

Among the huge whitetail hunting fraternity, the Mel Johnson typical whitetail is a true legend. Despite the enormous number of high-scoring whitetails taken and advances in archery equipment since 1965, Johnson's buck has remained as the No. 1 Pope & Young typical whitetail. In addition to the Sagamore Hill Medal, the trophy was also recognized by Pope & Young with its highest honor, the Ishi award.

Whitetail hunts tend not to be epic, but Johnson's hunt is a dream story of opportunity and maintaining one's composure while hunting with a bow and arrow. It is interesting to note that in a number of newspaper accounts of this buck, the deer's weight was listed at 270 pounds. It is fairly well known that whitetail body sizes increase the farther north one moves. However, a 270-pound whitetail is a huge deer anywhere!

From the *Arlington Heights Herald* (Arlington Heights, Illinois), Thursday, May 19, 1966:

Illinois, of course, doesn't have much of a reputation as a deer-hunting state, but one bow hunter—Mel Johnson of Peoria—will find that hard to accept.

He knocked down a 270-pound buck in Peoria County last October, striking the animal dead with one arrow fired from about 15 yards. This month, that bag was

rated by the Boone and Crockett Club as the most
outstanding of the 1,600 big game trophies submitted
to the club for consideration, and it won for Johnson
the 11th Sagamore Hill Medal awarded by the club
since 1948.

But more than that, the club—founded by Theodore
Roosevelt in 1887—scored the buck higher than a
Minnesota buck killed in 1918, which until 1966 was
rated as the world's finest whitetail trophy.

OFFICIAL MEASURER'S NOTE: An immense trophy taken with a recurve bow! Officially a 7x6 in terms of measurable points, the antlers lose only 1-1/8 inches due to a single non-typical point. Otherwise, long main beams of 27-5/8 inches (right antler) and 26-6/8 (left antler) are further enhanced by an impressive 23-5/8 inch inside spread. All but one circumference measurement exceed 5 inches, with both H1 measurements taping in excess of 6 inches. Lastly, the rack possesses five single tines in excess of 10 inches, with a sixth just under that at 9-7/8 inches.

1973 Sagamore Hill Medal – Doug Burris, Jr.
Mule Deer – 226-4/8

Doug Burris, Jr., was a trophy hunter, and had already taken at least two very fine mule deer on previous hunts before encountering his record deer in 1972.

At a score of 226-4/8, this buck remains the only typical mule deer netting over 220 inches. The buck's antlers, now owned by Cabela's, exceed the No. 2-ranking typical buck by a full 8 inches. Although it lacks the great mass of some of the other top-scoring mule deer trophies, its huge and artistically sweeping typical frame is unique and particularly beautiful.

The story of the Burris's hunt appeared in the 13th Edition of *Records of North American Big Game* published in 2011.

> Doug Burris, Jr., began hunting the Dolores County area of Colorado in 1969. On opening day of the 1972 season, Burris and his three companions, Jack Smith, Robbie Roe and Bruce Winters, piled into their Jeep before dawn and headed out.

> All the bucks the Texans saw that day were small and no one fired a shot. On the second day, Roe and Winters both took nice five-pointers, while Smith and Burris remained empty-handed. On the third day, Burris decided to go after a buck a friend had seen in Proven Canyon the day before. About mid-morning,

Burris spotted two nice bucks feeding in a clearing about 500 yards away. While he watched these two bucks, a third one came into view.

Burris knew immediately that the latter buck had to be exceptional as he could see antlers even without the aid of binoculars. He decided to make the stalk. For the better part of an hour, Burris slowly and quietly worked his way through the oak brush. About the time he felt he had cut the distance in half, he nearly stepped on a doe bedded down in the underbrush. She exploded out of the brush, and the three bucks Burris was stalking scattered in different directions. Burris had time for one quick shot with his .264 Winchester Magnum, and the largest buck crumpled in mid stride.

Upon closer examination, Burris realized he had an unbelievable trophy. In 1974, at the 15th North American Big Game Awards Program held in Atlanta, Georgia, Burris' World's Record was confirmed. With a final score of 225-6/8 points, Burris' buck took the first place award for the typical mule deer category in addition to the coveted Sagamore Hill Award for the finest trophy taken during that Entry Period.

When the so-called double-penalty was dropped for excessive spread at a later date by the Club's Records Committee, the final score of Burris' buck increased by 6/8 of an inch to score 226-4/8 points.

(Reprinted with permission from *Colorado's Biggest Bucks and Bulls*.)

OFFICIAL MEASURER'S NOTE: In addition to the comments above, it's worth noting that Burris's mule deer buck is one of the few with main beams at or near 30 inches on each side. In addition, the visual beauty of the antlers is enhanced by a 30-7/8-inch inside spread (the spread credit, which cannot exceed the length of the longer main beam, is 30-1/8 in the scoring calculation). The buck's G2s are amazing as well, and nearly identical in length, at 22-4/8 inches (right antler) and 22-3/8 inches (left antler). Three other points exceed 14 inches, and a fourth point measures a quarter-inch less at 13-6/8 inches.

Continue on to read more stories about the rest of the Sagamore Hill Award-winning trophies recognized by the Boone and Crockett Club.

When the Unexpected Happens

Garry Beaubien

British Columbia Mountain Caribou | Current Rank #3

T HE NEW WORLD RECORD MOUNTAIN CARIBOU, SCORING 452 points, was taken on the Turnagain River, B.C., on September 15, 1976, by Garry Beaubien.

The Beaubien party, including his father, his 12-year-old son, and his 13-year-old daughter, left Dease Lake on horseback on September 8, after a week of preparations. They were outfitted with four saddle horses and two pack horses. They headed east from Dease Lake in weather that remained beautiful the entire trip. Caribou were spotted on the second day out, so they made a good camp on the third day, hunting from there for two days. At this camp, they looked at two herds numbering 20 animals and more, each. Although there were some nice bulls, they were not the large ones that they were seeking.

CIRCA
1976

They broke camp after the second day's hunt, heading farther east. On the seventh day out, they left the main trail to move up a long side valley. There they spotted a herd with a huge bull, about five miles from them, up the side of the mountain. After looking the herd over with a spotting scope, they decided to make camp in order to try to get close enough to stalk the big bull.

Since it was still early in the afternoon, camp was quickly made and the pack horses were left in camp. They rode up the mountain, through heavy brush, until about 5 P.M. when they tied their horses and Beaubien and his father began their stalk.

The herd included 20 cows and 5 bulls, all feeding on the sidehill. The biggest bull was very impressive. Checking the wind, Beaubien and his father worked to within 200 yards. When the bull looked directly at them, Beaubien's father, who they had already agreed would take the shot, took careful aim and squeezed the trigger. The bull took two jumps and fell dead. Then, something totally unexpected happened.

From over a little knoll 200 yards to their left, 10 bulls appeared on the horizon, with a massive bull in the lead. After a quick look at Beaubien and his father, the huge bull led the other nine back over the ridge and out of sight.

Hardly believing what he had just seen, Beaubien ran to the knoll as fast as he could and looked over. The bulls were several hundred yards away, running up a side hill. They had only 200 yards to go before they would go over the mountain top forever. Quickly lying down on the knoll and putting the crosshairs of his scope on the top of the bull's shoulder, Beaubien waited for him to stop. When he did, Beaubien carefully squeezed the trigger. His father, watching through binoculars, cried, "You shot way low."

The bulls took off again for the top. The next time the bulls stopped they were just 100 yards from the summit. Beaubien aimed over the big bull's antlers and fired again. His father told him that he had still shot too low.

Beaubien's heart was pounding mightily as he waited, hoping for one last chance. The big bull stopped just as he reached the skyline, the nine other bulls strung out behind him. Holding well above him and right in the middle, Beaubien squeezed off his final effort, hoping that the 180-grain bullet from his .300 Winchester magnum would do the job. As the rifle report died, his father yelled, "You got him!"

The bull crumpled on the skyline, his back broken by the final shot. Beaubien and his father watched through their binoculars for several minutes to make sure that he was indeed down for keeps.

It took them three days of hard work to get the capes, meat and antlers back to Dease Lake. When they had stepped off the distance to Beaubien's trophy, it was 650 paces, a shot that in Beaubien's own words truly had some luck involved. Beaubien's father's trophy also turned out to be a very fine one, scoring 340 points.

Beaubien's caribou was recognized at the 16th North American Big Game Awards held in 1977 as the best in its category, and it was further honored with an award of the Sagamore Hill Medal.

Scoring 452 B&C points, Beaubien's trophy was second in the 1977 edition of the Boone and Crockett Club's records book to the long-standing world-record trophy taken by G.L. Pop in 1923.

OFFICIAL MEASURER'S NOTE: Here we get to do some additional compare and contrast, as we have the Deuling World's Record mountain caribou as well among the Sagamore Hill Award winners (see page 117 for his story). With Beaubien's bull, a picture is indeed worth a thousand words as seen on page 64). Perhaps a bit unfair (as the World's Record holds its own!), but just seeing a photo of the heavily-palmated top palms screams "huge." Indeed, the width of top palm measurements alone are roughly twice the dimensions of the equivalent measures for Deuling's bull. In addition, there are other key distinctions between the antler measurements of these two giant caribou. The Beaubien bull's inside spread credit, at 30-3/8 inches, is almost 10 inches narrower than that of Deuling's. Beaubien's also benefits greatly from the symmetry of its two rear points (those crazy single points that stick out from the back side of a caribou's main beam about halfway around the curve). Beaubien's bull's rear point difference (i.e. deductions) of 1-4/8 inches for asymmetry provide a large relative benefit versus the whopping 13-7/8 in deduction for Deuling's caribou (where right antler rear point length of 3-3/8 inches compares to 17-2/8 inches for the corresponding point on the left antler). In any event, the individual antler scores, before deductions and spread credit, for both of these magnificent bulls are at or in excess of 219 inches per antler!

The Longest Night

Michael J. O'Haco, Jr.

Arizona Pronghorn | Current Rank #5

IT WAS THE FIRST WEEKEND IN AUGUST 1985, AND I WAS OUT of town. I called home because I knew the Arizona hunting permits should be in the mail. My wife Linda said there was good news and bad news. I said I wanted the bad news first. She said that I had not received an elk permit. However, the good news was that I had received a deer and pronghorn permit. Already having a mule deer in the Arizona state records book, I was pleased at having drawn a deer permit, but not half as pleased as I was with the pronghorn permit. This was the 20th time I had applied for a pronghorn permit; the 19 previous times I had been rejected. The computer finally came through.

CIRCA
1985

After getting home, I called my hunting partner Phil Donnelly. We got together to plan how we were going to scout the unit we had been drawn for. Being a rancher in that same area, I would scout the top half of the unit, while Phil would scout the lower half. The top half was closer to where I was working cattle, and the lower half was closer to Winslow, where Phil lives. We met again after a couple of weeks and discussed what we had seen. He seemed to think that he had two records-book bucks in the lower half of the unit, and

[69]

I thought I had three records-book bucks in the top half, but one buck was exceptional.

I tried to get a look at the bucks Phil had spotted, but I was unable to find them. I kept track of two of the bucks I had spotted, but I couldn't find the big buck. I almost panicked! After a little research on pronghorn, I found that during early September in Arizona, a buck will be looking for his harem, but will return to his own territory after putting them together. The big buck did just that, and I found him again the week before the hunt. I explained to Phil where I had seen the buck the day before, and asked him to take a look. Phil came by the ranch that night and told me this definitely was the biggest buck he had ever seen. We agreed the buck would go high in the Boone and Crockett records book, but we didn't realize how high.

The afternoon and evening before the hunt, we decided to watch the big buck until he bedded down for the night. Phil watched until he couldn't see him in the spotting scope anymore, then he returned to the ranch. After supper, he explained to me exactly where the buck had bedded down. My family has ranched in this area for years, so I knew exactly where the buck was. We talked about using horses, or going in on foot, and if we should come in from the north or from the northeast. We decided that foot would be better, and that the northeast route would be the best. This way, we would have everything working for us, with the wind and the most cover, and also the sun at our backs.

Since this was my first pronghorn permit, I would get the first shot. If I missed, it was anybody's ball game. I had worked up a super accurate load of a Sierra 85-grain, hollow-point bullet, a Remington case and primer, and 41.5 grains of IMR 4350 powder. This load would be used in a Sako .243 rifle, with a 2–7x Leopold scope. I didn't intend to miss!

That night was one of the longest of my life, as my mind was filled with thoughts of the coming day's hunt on my mind. *Would the buck be there in the morning? Would we spook them before I could get a shot?*

Would I miss? Finally, about 3 A.M., I couldn't take it any longer. I got up and put the coffee on. Phil got up and asked how I felt. I said that as many times I had shot that pronghorn in my dreams, we should be able to drive out there and load him up.

We drove to within a mile of where the buck and his does had bedded down for the night. It was still an hour before daylight. We discussed how we would make our stalk, and tried to visualize all aspects of the stalk so there would be no mistakes.

Finally, it was light enough to make a move. We had to crawl over a fence and then use the scattered cedar trees for cover. We moved slowly. When we were about 300 yards from where we had seen them the night before, I spotted the does but couldn't see the buck. We crawled slowly and easily. When we were about 200 yards from the pronghorn, something caught my eye to the left. It was a buck. Phil was about 20 yards to my left. The buck was looking straight at me, with a slight right turn, and I could see just part of a shoulder. Not being able to tell if it was the big one, I whispered to Phil, "Is that him?" I knew the buck was big, but I couldn't see the prong from my angle.

Phil said, "That's him."

I shot. The buck broke and ran. I feared I had missed.

I jammed another shell into my rifle. I hollered at Phil to shoot. He said, "No, he's hit hard."

The buck slowed down, then stopped and looked back. I shot again, nothing. The adrenalin was really pumping through my body and I couldn't hold the cross hairs steady. Phil said to use his shoulder for a rest, but he was shaking worse than I was. I took a deep breath, got my composure, and squeezed. The buck finally went down and didn't get up.

When we got to the buck, we took a quick measurement and were awed by what we totaled. Two days later, I had Jerry Walters, an official Arizona state measurer, taped the buck at a green score of 95-2/8 points. The B&C Judges Panel at the 19th Big Game Awards Program measured my buck with a final score of 93-4/8 points.

A Good December

Charles E. Erickson, Jr.

Arizona Coues' Whitetail | Current Rank #5

FOR SEVERAL YEARS, I HAD BEEN HELPING A FRIEND OF MINE BY the name of Mick Holder with cow work and such on his ranch in Gila County, near Globe, Arizona. I have been in the cattle business most of my life and am an avid hunter. Until I met Mick, I had never been particularly interested in hunting *CIRCA* the Arizona Coues' whitetail deer. He had hunted them *1988* all his life and had guided for Coues' deer and black bear for many years. He had reached the point in his life where he did not care to guide anymore. He just enjoyed hunting with friends and interesting people he had met through the years. Mick is one of the keenest and most knowledgeable observers of nature I have ever seen.

Coues' deer season in Arizona generally takes place during the last half of December. The weather is cool to cold, depending on weather systems moving through the state at the time. December of 1988 was especially good, because we had several storms and a fair amount of snow at the higher elevations. Conditions were perfect to start the Coues' deer into the rut.

We hunted a few days in rain and fog, seeing lots of deer. I had in the past killed several nice Coues' bucks and was only interested in a good trophy. The country we like to hunt is rough, steep, rocky mountain sides. They have a good combination of browse and grass but not too much brush. We like to use spotting scopes as much as possible to save time and movement. Many times, I have walked right by smart bucks and have learned to glass them up first.

We prefer to hunt with 7mm magnums, because they provide the advantage of flat trajectory for a long shot if you are unable to make a close stalk.

The fourth day of the season, I was moving through some very rough, rocky draws. I had not been able to find anything suitable with my scope that morning and had no choice but to start moving. The bucks were holding tight. Crossing the series of draws was not easy since they are steep, and remaining silent is almost impossible.

Sure enough, I heard a few rocks roll above and ahead of me and got a good look at a fine trophy buck moving out of sight in a hurry. A quick test for a records-book buck is whether his antlers are wider than his ears and his rear tines are more than 6 inches long. This buck had them but was moving too fast and I couldn't get the shot.

I finished the day, met Mick that night, and told him what I had seen. We both agreed we should make another try for the buck the next day. There were no other hunters in the area, and we hoped he would stay close, so we could glass him. We planned the hunt that night, though we could not agree on how to do it. We had both hunted this mountain several times. He had his ideas; I had mine.

The next morning, we were on the mountain before daylight and had another parley on how to hunt that day. Mick told me that, from his years of experience with Coues' deer, he really did not think the buck would be where I thought he would be. I finally had to modify my plan and we started up the mountain. I went high, and Mick stayed below me.

The higher I climbed, the more draws and other likely hiding places I wanted to check out. Anybody who has hunted Coues' deer very long knows they will hold tight. I did not follow our plan and got behind the sweep we had planned to make across the face of the mountain. I knew I was behind and was mad at myself. Mick was out of sight, ahead and below me.

I had to cross a big, very steep rockslide. Trying to be quiet was almost impossible, but I crossed carefully and started to move forward. I had not taken three steps when a buck stood up. He was about 50 yards away and a little below me. He started running but not fast, down and away and to my right. When he first got up, I knew he was good, but when he moved a little and turned his head sideways, I could hardly see through his antlers.

Instantly, I sat down and took careful aim. My heart was in my throat as I squeezed off the shot. *Click.* I had forgotten to put a round in the chamber. I worked the bolt, thinking, "I'm going to get behind if I don't do it right."

I took careful aim again, fired and bolted in another round. He was still moving and about 80 yards away. I fired again and bolted in another round.

He kept running, but suddenly, he stopped about 125 yards away and looked back at me. I thought, "Boy, I've got to do it now."

I fired again. He turned and ran down the mountain into a draw, where he passed out of sight. I pulled one more round out of my pocket and put it into the chamber, throwing the balance of the cartridges in my pocket out on the ground so I could reach them quickly if I needed them. I waited for him to show himself crossing the draw, but he did not and I moved to check for blood. I found the blood trail. He had run another 50 yards and was lying in some rocks and tall grass.

I cannot repeat the words I said, but I was literally awestruck when I saw the antlers. I just sat down and stared. Finally, I noticed that I had hit him with all three shots. That made me feel better, because I never knew whether or not I was hitting him while shooting.

I stood up and began examining his antlers. One major drop tine had been broken but was still attached by old velvet. He either broke it when he fell, or he broke it fighting. I knew it would hurt his score.

It took Mick a while to get to me. When he arrived, his mouth dropped open, and neither of us could say anything. Finally, he said, "Erickson, it looks like you have had a good December."

We finished field-dressing the buck and started off the mountain. I fell into some prickly pear on the way down, which marred a perfect day and brought me back to reality. Nothing is perfect. Of course, the argument about the buck I had seen the day before started again. I finally agreed that Mick was right, as usual, but look at the result of my disagreement.

OFFICIAL MEASURER'S NOTE: As we noted elsewhere, some trophy antlers or horns just scream "exceptional" in photos. Many others don't—no matter how high their scores. This buck, in the writer's opinion, never fails to impress in photos or in antler configuration. It is true that large Coues' whitetail trophies tend to be impressive relative to the diminutive size of this subspecies, especially in terms of antler mass versus skull size. That all said, Erickson's award-winning (currently ranked No. 5) non-typical Coues' whitetail more or less has it all in terms of key visual attributes and scoring metrics. Namely, the buck possesses a strong inside spread credit of 16-6/8 inches. Only

Erickson Score 3-88B
Final Score #22
Short

OFFICIAL SCORING SYSTEM FOR NORTH AMERICAN BIG GAME TROPHIES

Records of North American Big Game

BOONE AND CROCKETT CLUB

P.O. Box 547
Dumfries, VA 22026

Minimum Score:	Awards	All-time
whitetail	185	195
Coues'	105	120

NON-TYPICAL
WHITETAIL AND COUES' DEER

Kind of Deer __COUES__

Abnormal Points	
Right Antler	Left Antler
5 1/8	4 3/8
3 1/8	1 3/8
6 3/8	2 4/8
1 3/8	
16 3/8	8 3/8
E. Total of Lengths of Abnormal Points	24 4/8

SEE OTHER SIDE FOR INSTRUCTIONS

				Column 1 Spread Credit	Column 2 Right Antler	Column 3 Left Antler	Column 4 Difference
A. No. Points on Right Antler	9	No. Points on Left Antler	8				
B. Tip to Tip Spread	11 5/8	C. Greatest Spread	20 0				
D. Inside Spread of Main Beams	16 5/8	(Credit May Equal But Not Exceed Longer Antler)		16 5/8			
F. Length of Main Beam					19 6/8	20 6/8	1 1/8
G-1. Length of First Point, If Present					3 5/8	4 8 1/8	4/8
G-2. Length of Second Point					9 5/8	9 9/8	6/8
G-3. Length of Third Point					8 6/8	4 3/8	4 3/8
G-4. Length of Fourth Point, If Present					2 4/8	4 7/8 5 1/8	2 3/8 5/8
G-5. Length of Fifth Point, If Present							
G-6. Length of Sixth Point, If Present							
G-7. Length of Seventh Point, If Present							
H-1. Circumference at Smallest Place Between Burr and First Point					4 7/8	4 5/8	2/8
H-2. Circumference at Smallest Place Between First and Second Points					4 7/8	4 9/8	2/8
H-3. Circumference at Smallest Place Between Second and Third Points					4 7/8	5 9/8	1/8
H-4. Circumference at Smallest Place Between Third and Fourth Points					5 2 5 4/8	4 7/8	1 5/8
TOTALS				16 5/8	63 3/8	60 4/8	10 7/8

Enter Total of Columns 1, 2, and 3	140 3/8	Exact Locality Where Killed:	16 5/8	62 3/8	60 7/8	9 6/8
Subtract Column 4	9 5/8 10 7/8	Date Killed:	By Whom Killed: #22 ERICKSON			
Subtotal	130 4/8	Present Owner:				
Add (E) Total of Lengths of Abnormal Points	24 4/8	Guide Name and Address:				
FINAL SCORE	153 7/8	Remarks:				

155 2 *Final Score* "
Eldon Buck Buckner
Final Score 5/6/92

B&C BIG GAME AWARDS 21 1989-1991

DETAIL OF POINT MEASUREMENT

a dozen other top Coues' deer trophies match or exceed that measure. The buck also has main beams approaching 20 inches each, which fairly equates to the 30-inch main beams found in top-ranking whitetail trophies. Lastly, Erickson's Coues' deer ranks just below the top 10 in terms of total length of the abnormal points which lend to the great aesthetic character of this buck. In particular, inward curving drop tines coming off both main beams give this particular deer its own unique visual appeal.

Brilliant Idea

Gernot Wober & Lawrence Michalchuk

British Columbia Rocky Mountain Goat | Current Rank #2

IT ALL STARTED ON SEPTEMBER 4, 1999, WHEN LAWRENCE Michalchuk needed to find a new goat hunting partner after his wife announced she could not accompany him on his next hunt. Lawrence and I have known each other for eight years and have spent many hours hunting and fishing together. I was not surprised to hear his voice on the other end of the phone. "Can you leave tomorrow?" he asked.

CIRCA
1999

Work was not a problem—I had been unable to find work as a mining exploration geologist for almost six months. But how was my relatively new girlfriend going to take the news that I was leaving that afternoon to go goat hunting? I put on my most loving attitude, drove to her shop at the ski resort, and mentioned my plans. Within the hour I phoned Lawrence to tell him I would arrive on Sunday at noon.

I drove nearly 500 miles from my home near Kamloops to reach Lawrence's home in Bella Coola, British Columbia. Not entirely prepared on such short notice, I borrowed longjohns, a backpack, Thermarest, raingear, and fleece pants to round out my skinny supplies. We packed homemade granola bars, trail mix, and Mr. Noodles packages for food, as well as a tent, small stove, and our bowhunting gear. Dividing the load between us, we each had approximately 60 pounds of gear to haul up the trail for a planned seven-day hunt.

From the trailhead, we slogged our way uphill for eight wet hours, climbing approximately 5,000 feet over five miles of trail. In retrospect, the only pleasant fact about the hike was that it was overcast and cool, and the view as we climbed out of the Bella Coola valley was spectacular. Low clouds draped themselves along the steep walls of the green valley and fog moved up and down the slopes as the wind changed.

The main Bella Coola Valley, which is tucked into the Coast Mountains about 250 miles west of Williams Lake, boasts some of the most magnificent views in British Columbia. Lush green valley bottoms host great salmon rivers such as the Atnarko and Talchako, where grizzly bear roam freely. Rows of large mountain peaks line the main valley, rising from sea level to over 8,000 snow-capped feet. Blacktail deer and mule deer follow trails along valleys and steep mountain slopes. Recently, the cougar population has been increasing and wolves seem to be thriving as well.

Canadian heritage abounds as one hikes along the nearby Alexander Mackenzie Trail. Native petroglyphs can be visited along Thorsen Creek, and the rock where Alexander Mackenzie carved his name in granite in 1793 can be reached by boat on the Bentick Arm from Bella Coola harbor.

We pitched our tent in what seemed to be the only dry 10 square feet for miles around. Fall rains had saturated the ground, and small lakes and ponds were everywhere. We were centrally located in an area that held Rocky Mountain goat, with only a few miles between the locations Lawrence wanted to check out. Lawrence had been up in this area hunting for goat numerous times and knew the terrain very well.

We had a few hours before dark so we pushed our weary legs a little farther, walked to the closest spot overlooking the Bella Coola Valley, and started glassing for goats. Along the edge of this east-west trending valley, it is very precipitous, well-vegetated, and perfect habitat for goat. We eventually spotted what looked to be a lone goat and probably a billy. We walked a small ridge parallel to the one the goat was on until we were 150 yards away from him. Lawrence put the spotting scope on the goat and said that it looked fairly large and was probably worth pursuing.

We both backed away slowly, walked around to the top of the ridge and started down to get closer. As we crept down small ledges without much cover, the goat spotted us and was staring directly at us from approximately 60 yards. Lawrence motioned that he was going to climb back up the ledges with the hope that the goat would watch him and allow me to get within bow range. The ruse seemed to work as I got to within 40 yards. I was directly above him with a steep downhill shot. As I made the shot, I saw the arrow sail directly for the goat and then deflect off a small tree just in front of him. I missed! The goat bounded down the rock walls into the steep gully.

Tuesday morning we debated whether we should go back after the same goat we had seen or try somewhere else. We decided to head north to a cirque in which Lawrence had seen lots of goat activity before. Two hours of fast walking found us along the edge of the very steep walled cirque from which we could glass a large valley. We spotted eight goats in pairs and singles on a number of different ridges and ledges well over a mile away. Several seemed quite large, although we were still too far away to be certain they were billies.

Unless we could get a lot closer, determining whether these animals were billies would be impossible. Both sexes have black, well-polished horns; the nanny's horns are generally longer with narrow bases and a wide spread, while the billy's have larger bases and heavier overall circumference measurements. On average, body size is not a reliable indicator. Later that day, Lawrence made a stalk on a goat that appeared to be a billy until the very last instant. I watched him creep toward the goat carefully trying to see over rises and rocks until he was within 10 yards of the animal. He took an arrow from his quiver, readied for the shot, and suddenly froze.

I took a step forward and realized, as Lawrence had, that this was a very large nanny.

By afternoon, we were quite a distance from camp so we thought it best to head back the way we came. We stopped to see if some of the goats we had spotted earlier had moved into a more favorable position. Looking over the steep edge on our side of the valley, Lawrence noticed a goat standing in thick brush approximately 50 feet up from the base of a cliff. As he looked through the scope, Lawrence said, "the bases of those horns are the biggest I've ever seen. Too bad we can't get to him from here."

We watched the big goat for a while and then headed back toward camp. At the time, neither of us knew we had spotted a potential world's record.

For the next two days we spotted and stalked numerous animals. I managed to deflect my arrows off more twigs and miss two shots on decent billies. At night as we cooked our meager dinners, all we could talk about was the large goat I had missed at the beginning of the hunt—aptly named Mr. Big—and the problems of accessing the area he was in. Lawrence was convinced that the goat was the largest he had ever seen in 16 years of hunting and I realized that thoughts of stalking it were consuming him. We discussed moving camp closer to the valley the goat was in but knew we couldn't climb down the cliffs at the headwall.

Friday morning brought a thick frost, but also the promise of sun for the first time in four days. After we had dried out and were comfortable again, we started hiking back to the truck. Lawrence and I had discussed things the evening before and reached a consensus that we should go after the big goat. The only way to get to him was to head home, get rid of most of our gear to lighten our loads, and start the grueling hike up the valley from the bottom. We headed to Lawrence's place looking forward to a change of socks, a hot shower, and to eating something other than sweet granola bars and Mr. Noodles.

The next day, we thrashed up a sidehill full of slide alder and devil's club for five hours to get up the new valley. Slide alder is nasty business. It grows sideways and upward 10 to 15 feet, and there is never a clearing through it—you simply climb on it or under it, often at the same time. Devil's club is aptly named for its toxic barbed needles that work their way into your skin until sufficient festering pops them out. As we had passed through a mature timber stand in the lower part of the valley, we noticed grizzly bear claw marks high up on the trees and clumps of hair stuck in the sap. It made us a little nervous, and we hoped the bear was in the lower valley looking for fish.

We almost turned back twice when the terrain and vegetation had us asking each other just what the heck we were doing here. *Whose brilliant idea was this anyway?* I pushed on, encouraging Lawrence to follow, but I was soon at wit's end and very frustrated with the thick brush. Next, it was Lawrence's turn to encourage me, pushing me to reach the next ridge. Finally, it appeared that the vegetation was giving way to rocky slide chutes, and we knew we were closer to our goal.

By noon, we were across the valley about a mile from the spot we had seen Mr. Big. At first we didn't see any activity, but as we were eating our lunch, Lawrence whispered, "He's there!"

We watched him in the spotting scope and were amazed once again at how obviously big the billy seemed. Another billy was about 500 yards up the valley from him and we noticed that both goats had been watching our progress up the south slope for quite some time. The large billy was in exactly the same spot where we had seen him days before.

Lawrence had his bow and I carried his .270. I had given up on bowhunting. We agreed that Lawrence would get the first shot with his bow and if he couldn't get a shot, I could try with his bow one more time or just shoot with the rifle. We dropped down to the valley creek where we cached our large packs next to some huge boulders, which served as a good landmark. After crossing the creek, we climbed up the slide, staying hidden in the slide alder, then proceeded on our hands and knees for about an hour through tall wet grass and stinging nettles. About 100 yards from where we last saw the goat, we noticed numerous trails and tunnels through the grass where he had been feeding. The billy had a veritable grocery store to feed from with very little competition. As luck would have it, he had come down off his perch and was feeding at the base of a cliff.

Lawrence took the lead with his bow and we continued forward even slower, keeping a willow bush between the goat and us. We arrived at the base of the cliff and there was no sign of the billy! We stared at each other for a second; not wanting to admit that we had spooked him then continued our stalk. Lawrence climbed up the cliff a little ways and then moved right, following some small ledges. I moved sideways and to the right, staying in the grassy talus so I could keep a larger area of the cliff in view.

Lawrence crossed above me to the right and started gesturing emphatically that the goat was right there in the thick bushes on the cliff. I couldn't see the billy yet so I scrambled up to where Lawrence was frantically pointing. I put the scope of the .270 up and sure enough I could make out the goat's vague outline at 70 yards. I told Lawrence I had a shot, though it was chancy through a bush. Lawrence told me to keep the scope on the billy, and he was going to try and sneak around the other side and get a bow shot at him. I watched Lawrence stalk around to the other side and then he went out of sight. Both the goat and I heard the muffled scrapes and rockfall that Lawrence couldn't help but make on the steep terrain.

After about 25 minutes of trying not to pull the trigger, I heard Lawrence yell, "Just shoot him."

Microseconds later the echo of the rifle shot was ringing through the valley and the goat dropped out of sight. All was silent.

"Did you get him?" Lawrence hollered.

"I think so," I replied, as I waited a minute longer to see if the goat was going to reappear for another shot.

As Lawrence climbed down from his perch, I crawled up on all fours to where I last saw the goat. The bed created by the goat was huge. We could have pitched a tent on the platform created in the bushes. The billy had obviously made this home for quite some time. He had an unrestricted view of most of the valley. I glanced over the edge of the bed and spotted the white fur of the goat in the bushes 10 feet below. I carefully scrambled down to him and poked him with the rifle to make sure he was dead.

I had not expected the body to be so large; the billy appeared to weigh between 350 and 400 pounds. The horns were bigger than anything I had seen in my short goat hunting career.

"Is it a small one?" Lawrence yelled from the base of the cliff. I knew he was being facetious—he knew it was a large billy, but just how big was the question.

All I could reply was, "Nope!"

Lawrence yelled back that he had just fallen 30 feet and didn't really feel like climbing up to where I was. "We've got to take the cape off up here so come on up," I shouted. By the time Lawrence scrambled his way up the cliff to where I was, I had tied a rope from a stunted spruce to the goat's head just to make sure we didn't lose it over the edge. "HOLY GOAT!" was all that Lawrence could say over and over again. "You don't know what you just shot!" was all the variation to the first theme that he could muster.

We took photos as best we could where the goat lay, as dragging the goat back up to his bed was impossible. We took the cape and the head off and let the body slip over the cliff. We clambered down the cliff to the goat's body and continued to roll the carcass all the way down to the creek in the valley bottom. We quickly deboned the hindquarters and took out the back straps, packing as much as we could carry. The blowflies found us right away and we had to fight to keep the eggs out of the meat. We carried the meat to our packs by the boulders and made camp under the overhang of the largest one. We started a fire and walked back to the goat carcass to pull off a rack of ribs and cut some steaks from the front end. Two hours later our socks were dry and we were feasting on what we knew was a very large goat.

Sunday morning we were well rested and ready for the long thrash back through the slide alder to get home. Five hours later, we made it to the truck and were on our way to Lawrence's home. After unpacking, I skinned out the goat's head and we green scored the horns. Knowing that the horns would shrink a little with drying, we conservatively measured the horns rounding some of the measurements downward. After we added all the totals and took off the deductions we ended up with a score of 58-2/8 points. The size of the billy we had just shot started sinking in after we realized that the goat might be in contention for the world's record.

After the compulsory 60-day drying period, an official measurer for the Boone and Crockett Club measured the horns. With an official score of 56-6/8 points, the goat tied the World's Record Rocky Mountain goat at the time, which was taken in 1949 in the Babine Mountains of British Columbia. What is intriguing is that the left horn had 1-1/8 inches broken off from the tip and could have scored even higher.

OFFICIAL MEASURER'S NOTE: As noted in our segment featuring Sagamore Hill Medal winners lacking detailed hunt stories (see Haase Rocky Mountain goat, specifically), Rocky Mountain goat horns don't offer the significant variety and wide differences in dimension we find in other species. The Wober-Michalchuk goat's overall score equates that of Haase's, tied for the No. 2 spot to share in the B&C records. The two SHA winning goats differ largely in horn length. Whereas Haase's goat horns measure precisely 12 inches per side, Wober-Michalchuk's trophy horn measurements are 11-7/8 and 10-6/8 inches. Had this almost 1-inch difference not been the case, the Wober-Michalchuk goat's score could have arguably and handily exceeded that of Haase's, all other things being equal.

FINAL ~~Rot~~ 5/3/01
05-7-204
Fred J. King

Records of
North American
Big Game

250 Station Drive
Missoula, MT 59801
(406) 542-1888

BOONE AND CROCKETT CLUB®
OFFICIAL SCORING SYSTEM FOR NORTH AMERICAN BIG GAME TROPHIES

MINIMUM SCORES		
AWARDS	ALL-TIME	
47	50	

ROCKY MOUNTAIN GOAT

1st AW
Sagamore Hill
World Record, tie

B&C BIG GAME AWARDS
24
1998 - 2000

SEE OTHER SIDE FOR INSTRUCTIONS	COLUMN 1	COLUMN 2	COLUMN 3
A. Greatest Spread	8 7/8	Right Horn	Left Horn	Difference
B. Tip to Tip Spread	8 2/8			
C. Length of Horn		11 7/8	10 6/8	1 1/8
D-1. Circumference of Base		6 4/8	6 4/8	- 0 -
D-2. Circumference at First Quarter	2 31/32	5 2/8	5 2/8	- 0 -
D-3. Circumference at Second Quarter	5 15/16	3 4/8	3 4/8	- 0 -
D-4. Circumference at Third Quarter	8 29/32	2 1/8	2 1/8	- 0 -
TOTALS		29 4/8	28 3/8	1 1/8

ADD	Column 1	29 4/8	Exact Locality Where Killed: BELLA COOLA, B.C.
	Column 2	28 3/8	Date Killed: 9-12-99 Hunter: Gernot Wober
	Subtotal	57 7/8	Owner: Gernot Wober Telephone #:
SUBTRACT Column 3		1 1/8	Owner's Address:
FINAL SCORE		56 6/8	Guide's Name and Address:

Remarks: (Mention Any Abnormalities or Unique Qualities)
Bullet Hole at Right Base, Left Tip Broked

I, Ronald L Sherer, certify that I have measured this trophy on 05-02-01
at Bass Pro Shop
STREET ADDRESS   CITY   STATE/PROVINCE
and that these measurements and data are, to the best of my knowledge and belief, made in accordance with the instructions given.

Witness: albert eglat E015   Signature: Ronald L. Sherer   I.D. Number 5069

COPYRIGHT © 2000 BY BOONE AND CROCKETT CLUB®

[87]

Going Solo

Harvesting a trophy-class animal is one thing; tackling the adventure alone adds a whole other element of intrigue to the story. These hunters took to the mountains with only their outdoor skills and experience as their hunting partners. For many seasoned sportsmen, this is the only way they'd have it. A true test of one's mettle, indeed.

The Old Warrior

Fred Peters

Arizona Black Bear | Current Rank #39

C ENTRAL ARIZONA MAY SEEM AN UNLIKELY PLACE TO HUNT black bear, but bear do inhabit the brush and cactus covered mountains and canyons, and an inordinate number of them reach the huge proportions that hunters dream about. Maybe it's the mild winters and abundant feed, or being able to reach a ripe old age in an isolated area, but for whatever reason, there are some enormous bears in Arizona.

CIRCA
1985

Ingrained in the Southwest is a long and deep tradition of hunting bear with hounds. Many of the greatest of the lion and bear hunters, men like Ben Lilly and Monteque Stevens, Uncle Jimmy Owens and Homer Pickens, the Goswicks, the Evans, the Lee brothers, and many others, did their hunting in the rugged southwestern mountains. Theodore Roosevelt made numerous trips to Arizona and Colorado to hunt bear and lion behind a pack of local hounds. And even today, there is some fine bear hunting within sight of Zane Grey's cabin, where the author wrote many of his western novels, and chased bear and lion with hounds. A man riding these hills today is following in some famous footsteps as he pursues his elusive quarry.

My own pack of seven dogs is a mixture of redticks and blueticks, out of the big game hounds of Clell and Dale Lee. I was fortunate to have hunted with Clell and Dale, and I learned by their example the meaning of persistence and long rides, of fair chase ethics, and true hounds. Bear hunting from horseback, using dogs in the dry and rocky southwest, is an uncertain and sporting proposition.

I live in Show Low, Arizona, and have hunted for bear and lion with hounds for the past 16 years, mostly on the White Mountain Apache Reservation. This 1.7 million-acre reservation is famous for the trophy elk taken annually from the high, aspen and pine covered ridges, and there is also good hunting for deer, bear, lion, and javelina.

One day in October 1984, my son Joe and I decided to hunt some of the pinyon-juniper country that borders the Salt River Canyon, where I had found a particularly large bear track the previous spring. Cut a small section out of the Grand Canyon and drop it in central Arizona, you'd have a fair replica of the Salt River Canyon. It is this type of ruggedness that discourages hunters and, we hoped, had allowed some bears to grow both old and big.

The third day we hunted, the dogs trailed a giant bear track into an impossibly rough, rocky canyon where the bear whipped the dogs and escaped. Joe and I, our horses and our hounds, were physically beat as we limped back to camp by moonlight. But, we resolved to regroup and try that big, mean bear another day.

In the spring of 1985, despite numerous hunts in the Salt River area, we were unable to locate the big bear. The weather had been relatively dry, so we did most of our scouting near sources of water. At one of the cattle water catchments we found the big bear's impressive tracks. We did not find enough sign to know his exact habitat, but at least he was still alive and in the area. Not far from the water catchment was a suitable campsite with an old corral and water for our horses. The road into camp was difficult and steep, but we figured we could pull the horse trailers in by using four-wheel drive, if the weather stayed dry. We made our plans for a three-day hunt in early September. I would hunt the first day alone, and Greg and his son would haul in additional horses and camp gear for the next two days.

It was cool in the early morning darkness as I loaded my hounds and horses. Show Low is over 6,000 feet in elevation, but our campsite, 45 miles from town, was about 1,000 feet lower, and much warmer. In September it is sometimes too warm, as the hounds run out of gas quickly in hot weather, leaving only the cool, early morning hours to hunt effectively. By the time I arrived at our campsite, dawn was breaking. I hurriedly saddled my big brown horse, while the dogs whined impatiently in their boxes. The first place to check was the cattle tank where we had found the big bear's track in August.

The dogs detected no scent at the tank, so we continued down the crooked ravine that drained from the cattle tank. A mile or so down the ravine, we climbed out and headed across a series of ridges and canyons. As I rode into one particularly rugged canyon, the dogs started drifting ahead with their heads up and noses quivering, as they searched the air currents for the scent of bear. Just as they reached the bottom, my big redtick hound, Bart, announced with a bellow that he had found a bear. Immediately, the other six hounds joined in. With an excited chorus of barks, the dogs roared up the twisted canyon. These canyons are also inhabited by Coues' whitetail deer and javelina, which my young dogs will sometimes chase, so I leaped off my horse to try to find a track. In the gravel where the dogs had barked was a single large, flattened-out area. Not really much to go on, but it was a bear, and a big one, and the dogs were going in the right direction.

By the time I had remounted and urged my horse forward, the baying of the dogs had faded into the distance. My big horse, a veteran of many bear hunts, dodged between rocks and trees as he rushed after the dogs. For a long time, my goal was simply to hold on and not get wiped off by branches or brush. At the same time, I tried not to lose the distant sound of the baying hounds.

I would ride rapidly for a quarter-mile or so, then stop and listen for the dogs. This stop-and-go procedure continued for quite a while, until one of the times I paused to listen I thought the dogs sounded louder. Then, within minutes, I could hear clearly the

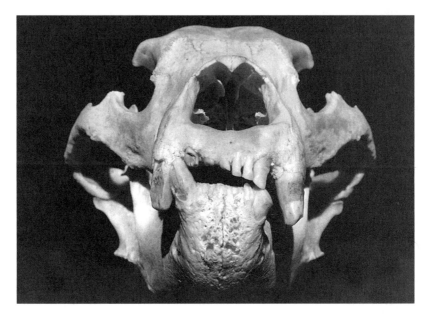

excited barking, mixed with angry growls. The dogs had jumped the bear, and he was headed back down the canyon in my direction. I quickly dismounted, and withdrew my Model 99 Savage in .250 caliber from its scabbard.

As the furious sound of the hounds came closer, I searched for movement. Finally, I saw him, a huge black bear running easily ahead of the dogs. But, before I could get the rifle up, he was hidden by juniper trees and then was gone on down the canyon, the dogs thundering behind him. From my brief glimpse, I could tell that he was indeed a big bear. But, he was more of a lean, raw-boned fighter, not a fat, roly-poly butterball. He was remarkably tall, and he ran effortlessly. This could be a long chase.

Again my horse carried me at a fearful rate between boulder and branch as we plunged down the canyon after the bear and hounds. For a time, we held our own, but it gradually became apparent that we were falling farther behind. Despite our best efforts, the bear was getting away and the dogs would soon be out of hearing. From a high vantage point, I could barely discern some faint echoes as the dogs and bear were swallowed up by the immense Salt River

Canyon. And then, when all appeared lost, there was a strange silence. For a long minute, I strained to hear above the breeze, until finally a solitary bark emanated from the distant chasm. Then, there was another bark, and another, until there was a thunderous roar from the depths of the canyon. The bear had treed!

I couldn't believe my good fortune! I rode rapidly to get closer. From a promontory, I could see a solitary ponderosa pine in the canyon bottom. The excited chorus was coming from it.

About 400 yards from the tree, I dismounted and, leaving my horse, approached the tree from downwind with a cartridge chambered in my rifle. When approaching a treed bear, it is best to keep out of sight and smell until you can dash under the tree; this helps keep the bear up in the tree. There can be real havoc if a bear comes down into a pack of dogs who are trying to impress their owner. It's the bear who usually makes the biggest impression.

Luck was with me that day, as I was able to approach within 40 yards undetected, then rushing under the tree before the huge bear could decide what to do. He was standing on his hind legs on a limb about 15 feet off the ground, and he would occasionally emit a low rumbling growl and snap his cavernous jaws. Immediately, I knew that this bear was one of the big boys. Even though he was not fat, there was no doubt that he was a tremendous bear with an awesome head and neck, and formidable, pile-driver front feet. He appeared to be an old bear, well past his prime, but still in good shape and the obvious kingpin of this area. I had a momentary impulse to tie the dogs and let this old warrior go. But, this was the bear of a lifetime, so I raised my rifle.

After he was dead, I sat for a while and admired him, alone with my dogs and my thoughts. I was feeling proud that I was able to catch this old monarch. But, I was also melancholy that my sons weren't here to share this moment, and that by killing this old bear, there would be a void in these hills and canyons. Perhaps we, as hunters, need to dwell more upon these things. Happily, there were to be many more hunts with my sons, and bears to take the place of Old Big Boy.

The King

Lester M. Miller

Washington Columbia Blacktail | Current Rank #1

FROM THE VERY FIRST MOMENT THAT I SAW THIS BUCK, I KNEW I had to have him, no matter the cost in time or effort.

He was standing at the back-end of an open hay field, near a patch of second growth timber. His horns glistened in the morning sun and he looked almost like an elk. I had been walking up an old railroad grade that was half obscured by willow and alder. It appeared that I might be able to get close enough for a clear shot at him, but that was not to be. I was carrying my Winchester Model 1894 .30-30 carbine, not capable of making clean kills at any great distance. My deer hunting had been limited to heavy brush shooting at ranges of 150 yards or less, and this big buck stood at least 300 yards away. I carefully moved to a small opening and pecked out. The buck either saw me or heard me. He was into the second-growth in a flash.

CIRCA *1953*

For the greater part of every day of every legal hunting season in the years of 1950, 1951, and 1952, and until that all-important day in October 1953, I stalked, drove thickets, and took stands in the Upper Lincoln Creek Area of Lewis County, Washington.

On as many as a dozen different occasions during that period, we were able to see him in the vicinity of Lincoln Creek. At Grange meetings, livestock auctions, and wherever people gathered in the nearby towns of Chehalis, Centralia, Fords Prairie, or Adna, it was not unusual to hear someone mention this majestic animal. Mostly, they would talk about his huge antlers, four points or bigger. Of course, the stories grew in the telling and soon he was almost a legend. Although I had twice jumped this deer out of his bed, and had seen him running down a runway on three or four different occasions, I still had never fired a shot at him, fearful that I might wound him and not make a clean kill.

And so it went. The sightings continued to be reported, with an occasional shot fired at the buck. He was seen often in the company of two other large bucks in late summer and early fall. He was seen in many different places (sometimes at the same time), from Doty Lookout to Adna, up Bunker Creek Road to Lincoln Creek. To hunt and to take this fine buck became an obsession with me. As the 1953 season approached a gnawing kind of fear grew in me that a poacher might kill him or someone else would get him during the coming season.

I began to look for him on foot before the season—cold-tracking him mostly, but many times hot on his trail. The purpose of this was for me to get familiar with his whereabouts and his habits, and hopefully to catch a glimpse of him and rid myself of a little of the "buck fever" I usually felt when I would see him. I covered a lot of ground during this period as I was not hampered by carrying a gun or being heavily dressed. This game came to an end two days before the general buck season opening in 1953. For the greater part of that day, I had been traveling along the creek bottoms and alder swamps, hoping to cut sign.

The day was rainy and the brush was wet. I was wearying of the game, when right in front of me in the muddy crossing, I saw the unmistakable tracks of several large deer and one smaller one.

My pace quickened as I began to follow the very fresh tracks. They led me up the side of a small hog-backed ridge, covered with thick hemlock. I worked my way through this wet brush and merged on the other side to look down into a large, open alder bottom. There, not 50 yards away, were two large bucks, one a fork-horn and one a very nice four-point. But the size and majesty of a third buck dwarfed the other two. Here was my prize buck! He was nuzzling the neck of a young doe, occasionally watching the other two deer as they sparred with each other.

As quietly as I could, I worked myself back into the heavy cover and made my way down to the creek bank where I sat down. I noticed that my hands were trembling and they continued to do so for some time. Naturally, my mind was full of thoughts and plans for opening day of the buck season, just 36 hours away.

My plan for the hunt was fairly simple. As I saw it, I would drive up the forestry road to a point where I could park. As soon as it was daylight, I would walk to the creek, which I felt certain would be an excellent place to start hunting. However, I reasoned that those deer could move some distance in any direction since my sighting of them two days before. Daylight found me parked on the forestry road, preparing to enter the woods. My pack contained a hatchet, knife, whetstone, rope, first-aid kit, lunch, a water-proof tube of matches, a liver bag, and a handful of .30-30 shells.

Arriving at the crossing where I had picked up the tracks before, I discovered more tracks in the mud. They indicated that the deer had returned on their back-track to this creek bottom. It took me quite awhile to figure out the direction the deer had gone when they left the bottom. After several false starts, I finally found the right trail and proceeded to follow the tracks. The deer were obviously following a well established game trail to another locality.

Although it was once again raining and any sounds I made were muted, it was difficult to travel this muddy runway without making considerable "sloshing" sounds. I had left the runway, walking in moss, grass and rotting wood parallel to it, when I rounded a bend in the trail and found myself face-to-face with a huge four-point buck. He was no more than 25 feet from me! I don't know to this day what kept me from shooting that deer. He was a prize in any man's language. I guess instinctively I must have known that he wasn't the one. He whirled around and bounded 30 feet away to the creek, jumped it, and disappeared into the woods.

At the same time, a short way up the creek, I saw the ghostly figures of two other deer cross the creek and disappear. The relatively small clearing in which I was standing came to an abrupt end about 50 yards upstream. At that point, a fringe of sapling spruce made— almost solid wall. The runway went through this spruce thicket. As I moved up to peer through it, I saw the rump of a very large deer disappearing up the trail. I bent over and began to trot as best as I could after the now-running animal. My pursuit slowed, faltered, and came to a stop after a time, as I became winded and needed rest. I felt that unless the deer entered a clearing or an area of sparse timber, and stopped, I had lost him.

As I sat there, I could see a fairly high ridgetop over the alder trees and what appeared to be an opening on the side of the ridge. I got to my feet and began making my way toward that clearing. It was only about 150 yards through the bottom to the base of the ridge. When I arrived at the opening, I found that the clearing had been created by a massive debris torrent. Supersaturated dirt and debris had let go and slid down the ridge. In the middle of the clearing, 80 yards away, stood my buck! He was quartering away from me, looking downhill right at me. I raised my gun and fired. The bullet struck him behind the shoulder and went into the head. He went down in his tracks and never moved.

I have killed many bull elk in my lifetime. But, no animal has ever had the impact on me that this huge buck had when I looked down on him as he lay there on the side of that ridge.

The antlers were awesome to see with their spread and color and symmetry. In addition, they were hanging heavy with moss and lichen that he had accumulated while feeding or "horning" the alders and willows along the creek.

I placed the Game Department seal on a horn and field dressed him, putting the liver and heart in my liver bag. With my hatchet, I cut alder poles, turning the carcass belly-down on them to cool-out while protected from the rain.

With one last look at my magnificent (to me) buck, I hurried downstream to try and get help to get him out to the road. By my reckoning, the road was about three miles away.

Although this hunt took place decades ago, certain things are as clear now in my mind as they were then: the first time I saw him; the times he out-smarted me; and, of course, the day his luck ran out.

One of the things that keeps the hunt fresh in my mind is the neverending stream of visitors that come to see and admire "The King", and the letters I have received from those who have pursued him in vain.

27 Years Later

Gene R. Alford

Idaho Cougar | Current Rank #2

EDITOR'S NOTE: The following article was written by George Bettas for Boone and Crockett Club's 25th Big Game Awards *book and includes a portion of Harold Nesbitt's original article that appeared in a 1989 issue of the* Boone and Crockett Associate's Newsletter. *Photographs courtesy of George Bettas.*

For only the 14th time, the Boone and Crockett Club awarded its highest award, the Sagamore Hill Award, to a trophy representing the highest attainment of sportsmanship and Fair Chase at the 20th North American Big Game Awards on June 10, 1989. The award was presented to Gene Alford of Kamiah, Idaho, for his cougar scoring 16-3/16 points that is second only to the World's Record in the category. Alford's story embodies the best of the sporting tradition that the Boone and Crockett Club has always encouraged and recognized with its records keeping for native big game of North America.

I met Gene Alford for the first time on June 8, 1989, at the 20th North American Big Game Awards in Albuquerque, New Mexico. He was very reserved and on the bashful side but I found him to be a tremendously interesting and knowledgeable person as I engaged him in a number of discussions about everything from

CIRCA
1988

cougar hunting to packing into the backcountry with horses and mules. As a result of our meeting in Albuquerque I became well enough acquainted with Gene that he invited me to bring my horses and mules and join him for two different 100-mile pack trips into Idaho's Selway-Bitterroot Wilderness. I made the first trip with Gene in August 1989 and the second trip two years later with Gene and my two daughters. These trips afforded me the opportunity to engage in many wonderful conversations with Gene, but most of all I got to know him as a person and developed a great appreciation for Gene as a hunter, woodsman, and outdoorsman.

There are generally two schools of thought when it comes to horse/mule packing. You either pack with a sawbuck pack saddle and hang your gear on the pack saddle securing it with a mantie and a diamond hitch or you use a decker saddle and mantie up your loads and secure them to the pack saddle with a basket hitch or a similar hitch. Gene's packing technique involves placing equal amounts of gear in manties, folding the mantie around the load and using a carefully tied rope to hold the load together. Each mantied load is then put on the decker with a basket hitch. I was intrigued by Gene's careful, methodical, step-by-step manner of placing his gear in manties, tying them neatly together, and attaching them to the decker with nary a wasted movement. Each day we would put the stock out to feed at daylight, cook our breakfast, pack our gear, load the stock and ride to a new destination. Upon our arrival we would put the stock out to graze, set up the wall tent, build a fire in the wood stove and cook supper. After supper we had a great time just talking. I spent most of my time simply listening to Gene's accounts of many different hunts and backcountry experiences. The first trip was a special learning experience for me. Gene's outdoor skills were apparent at every turn in the trail. From atop his Tennessee Walker mule he would note interesting tidbits of information ever so often as we made our way through the wilderness. He was especially cognizant of wildlife movement in the area but also pointed out interesting historical and geographical features. His dogs, Kelly and Scratch, accompanied us on the first trip. These were the two dogs that he hunted cougar with in the Selway each February and were the dogs that treed his big cougar. Gene described Scratch as a "mostly blue-tick" hound. Kelly was a Kelpie which is a working dog well-suited to most livestock working situations. The Working Kelpie has been in North American since shortly after the turn of the century. Gene had an interesting way of "hitching" Scratch and Kelly together with a short tether. Since the dogs were allowed to run at will along with the pack string a fresh cougar or bobcat track could present a problem if Scratch chose to pursue the cat. Kelly served as an "emergency" brake for Scratch. On one occasion we did cut a fresh cougar track on the trail. Gene noticed it in the dust from his mule. Scratch launched on the track with a howl and a burst of speed, but when Gene called to Kelly, she simply sat down and put on the brakes. After a bit of tugging, Scratch knew what the plan was and soon both Scratch and Kelly were loping along in unison with the pack string.

When we arrived at our evening campsites Gene would tie Scratch on a rope out of the back of the wall tent so he could come into the tent or stay outside as he wished. Kelly was allowed to spend her time as she chose until the next morning when we were ready to hit the trail again. As the horses and mules were saddled and packed, Kelly would always anticipate the moment when Gene would take Scratch off his tether and call for her. Inevitably she would be hiding nearby, not all that excited about being Scratch's "brakes" for the day. After a bit of coaxing she always came out of hiding, to be hitched to Scratch and off they would go in lock step down the trail.

The second summer was even more special for me as my two daughters, Ashley and Elizabeth, accompanied us on the pack trip. Although Gene was a bachelor with no children, he was an immediate hit with the girls. He patiently answered their questions and showed them how to do many "little" things with their horses. The down side of the trip was that Scratch had died the previous winter and was not with us. Gene had a new "mostly blue tick" pup along that was learning to be an all around cougar dog. He assigned the chores of feeding and caring for his new pup on the trip to Elizabeth. The grin on her face was evidence that she enjoyed the assignment.

My children and I had a unique opportunity to share time together with Gene Alford on these trips. We learned a great deal from Gene, but most of all, I came to appreciate the wealth of Gene's outdoor skills and his innate ability to work with animals. He had a special talent when it came to horses, mules, dogs and the wilderness. He was simply the consummate outdoorsman in the truest sense of the word.

Gene Alford moved to Idaho in 1959 to work for an outfitter, guiding hunters in the Selway River area. He had always loved hounds and cougars, and had spent many years hunting cougars with his strike dogs in California. The cougar hunting skills he had perfected in California served him well when he moved to Idaho's Selway Country. Before long Gene discovered that he had found a pretty close approximation to "cougar paradise." Idaho is great cougar country, with plentiful food (deer, elk, and other game) and great cover provided by mountainous areas with limited access for motorized vehicles. Before long he took up residence in Kooskia, (pronounced KOOS-key), nestled amid protective hills at the confluence of the Southfork and Middlefork of the Clearwater River at the gateway to the Selway-Bitterroot Wilderness. While living there and guiding in the backcountry, Gene soon found a great way to spend a month each winter, hunting cougar with his dogs. Gene's annual cougar hunt evolved into a regular feature on his yearly calendar.

Each February, he would hire a local pilot to fly him, with his dogs and gear, into a campsite along the Selway River in the Selway-Bitterroot Wilderness. There, he would set up camp and let each day's agenda be determined by the cougar sign he and his dogs found on his daily hunting routes. Gene chose the month of February because, in his experience, he had learned that during February

Gene with his dogs and packtrain traveling through a remote, mountain air strip.

there were concentrations of big game animals—especially whitetail deer—along the Selway River, which attracted good numbers of cougar. The weather along the river during February was generally better than the earlier months and facilitated more days of hunting.

You should understand that Gene Alford was no spring chicken when he took this record-book cougar. He was 66 years old at the time. A lot of folks at that age are concerned about a trip to the library on a snowy day, let alone being put out on their own in a wilderness area, with only two dogs for companionship, for a month. But, at the time of his hunt Gene was more than up to the task. He was in excellent physical condition, with a wiry build and the slight squint of the Westerner who has spent a great many days afield under the blazing sun. And he had been chasing big cougar in this fashion for nearly 30 years.

Interestingly, Gene felt that the weather conditions are the most serious health hazards to be faced on his winter outings. With the ever-present snow and ice, a fall resulting in broken limbs and severe impairment of function could be fatal. So, Gene exercised caution and good sense, including using ice cramp-ons on his boots to avoid slipping on icy surfaces.

Gene brought some big cougars to bay in his years of hunting in this fashion. In 1961, he killed two big toms that were entered in the Boone and Crockett Club's records program with the same score, 15-12/16 points, both equal to the score of the then World's Record. The scores of both were found to be slightly smaller by the Awards Judges Panel, but both were given the same final score, 15-11/16 points, and entered into the 1964 records book as tied (with two others at the same score) for number 3 for the category. A lesser hunter might well have hung-up the ice cleats and gun after this accomplishment, but not Gene Alford. He continued his yearly hunts, treeing a great many cougar and simply photographing or looking at most of them before letting them go; he was after a really big one.

Part of Gene's resolve to continue after a big one was disappointment in his two cougars ending up as only number three for the category after the initial entry score indicated they would tie the long-standing record, which was Theodore Roosevelt's cougar taken in 1901 near Meeker, Colorado.

At that same competition (as the awards programs were called in those days), a cougar entered by Ed Burton and taken in 1954 scoring 15-12/16 points, tied the World's Record. In those days, communications were not as good as today. Gene did not attend the competition, and he had to rely on information relayed to him with the return of his skulls. Apparently that information failed to properly settle questions in Gene's mind as to how his two skulls dropped in score and in potential rank, giving him additional incentive to find another, bigger tom.

Interestingly, Burton's cougar may have been even larger had not a sloppy field-dressing job with an ax removed an estimated 2/16 inch from the skull length.

Similarly, one of Gene's cougars was missing a portion of the back of its skull as well. At the time Gene hunted with a .38 pistol and accidentally shot one of these record cats at the base of the skull, destroying part of the skull resulting in a significant loss of skull material and a lesser skull length. Today Gene hunts with a scoped .357 pistol and does not have to worry about an errant bullet hitting a cougar in the wrong place.

Of course, back then, only the material present and unaltered on a trophy could be officially measured. So, Burton's trophy simply tied the World's Record instead of setting a new standard. Gene's damaged cougar skull was similarly scored and his trophy likewise scored lower than it would have if all of the skull material had been present. In any event the harvesting of these exceptional cougars certainly did indicate that there were some big toms out there.

Gene found what may well be his ultimate cougar on February 26, 1988. His hound, Scratch, struck the tom's trail at 8 A.M. that morning. Gene's hunting technique is different from what most cougar hunters are used to in areas where cougar are hunted during the winter when snow is present. Gene described the dogs and the technique used by most hunters as "turn in" hounds/hunting. What he means is that the hunters locate a cougar track by driving a vehicle or snowmobile along backcountry roads until they locate a cougar track. When they find a track they assess the freshness of the track and attempt to determine the size of the cat by the size of the track. When a suitably fresh and sizeable track is found the hunters "turn in" their dogs on the track, making sure that the dogs follow the track in the direction in which the cat is traveling.

Gene hunted with a "strike dog" and believes this method of hunting is more challenging and demanding since the hunter is

Gene Alford donated the cougar skull to the Boone and Crockett Club's National Collection of Heads and Horns, which is on display at the Buffalo Bill Historical Center in Cody, Wyoming.

on foot and the dog is allowed to range ahead of the hunter as the hunter courses through the country. Gene perfected this method of hunting cougar while he was in California where there was seldom any tracking snow and cougar were hunted on dry ground. Gene would also tell you that hunting cougar in snow is much easier than hunting on bare ground, requiring more highly trained dogs with excellent noses. The other interesting aspect of Gene's hunting technique on this hunt is that his second dog, Kelly, was not a hound but a Kelpie—a stock dog much more often found on a ranch than on cougar hunts. When Scratch struck a cougar track, Kelly was right on his heels during the chase with all the enthusiasm for chasing the cat that she would have for chasing a rank old range bull out of the brush on a hot summer day.

Gene's hunting involved hiking through deer winter ranges at elevations ranging from 2,000 feet to more than 7,000 feet. When the dog "strikes" a cougar track the dog pursues the track, and sometimes follows the track in the wrong direction because the dog is not under the immediate control of the hunter who can see what direction the cat is traveling. On other occasions the strike dog will pick up a cougar track on ice or frozen ground where no tracks are visible. In either case the strike dog pursues the cat and the hunter follows until the cat is treed, the scent lost or until the hunter can get the dog turned around if it is backtracking.

Gene knew the crossing points of the cougar in the area he hunted and noted that the old toms travel in circles, making the circuit in about two weeks. The cats do this so as to continually be hunting undisturbed game and not push the game from the area.

In the case of Gene's record cougar he, Scratch, and Kelly picked up the track in a saddle at about 3,500 feet in elevation. Scratch began cold trailing the track with Kelly in pursuit as well. After an hour of cold trailing and a considerable amount of gain in elevation Gene found one of the cougar's tracks in a patch of soft snow under a fir tree. The dogs were headed in the right direction but they were still cold trailing! Three hours after the trail had been cut, Gene found himself on top of a 6,000-foot ridge with the dogs following the cat's trail down the other side. Just a short distance down the back side of the mountain the dogs jumped the cougar. Fortunately for Gene and his dogs, the cougar only went about halfway down the mountain before, in Gene's words, "Stepping up the first tree it came to." A very tired Gene rested before taking some pictures and then using his .357 pistol to shoot the huge tom. It was when he started to skin the cat that he realized just how big-bodied this cougar was. It was so heavy that Gene couldn't lift the hindquarters to aid his skinning. It was obviously heavier than the normal 200 pounds of a really big tom cougar.

It was estimated by Gene and others that the big tom must have weighed about 225 pounds, a real monster cat. Gene recalled quite vividly just how heavy the skin and skull were; they weighed 42 pounds when he got back to his camp, a real load under the weather conditions and after the day's long and tiring chase.

After the required 60-day drying period, Gene had the skull measured officially for entry into the Boone and Crockett Club's 20th Awards Program. Just as in 1961, the entry score tied the current World's Record score. Would this be history repeating itself? Yes it would, but with a much more pleasant ending.

The score for entry was 16-4/16 points, placing it in an apparent tie with the World's Record taken by Douglas E. Schuk in 1979. The 20th Awards Final Judges Panel scored Gene Alford's trophy as 16-3/16 points, not a tie for the World's Record but clearly the new All-time number 2 for the category. And in view of the great number of years of hunting by Alford with a lofty goal of trophy quality, the personal sacrifice to hunt with just his dogs each year, and the details of an excellent, Fair Chase hunt and kill, this trophy was a top contender for the coveted Sagamore Hill Award. This time Gene would not have any questions about the process and the recognition for his trophy. However he would tell you that a question still lingers in his mind, he boiled the skull to clean it and may have boiled it longer than he needed to, thereby causing the skull to shrink more than it would have if beetles or a maceration chamber had been used to clean it.

In his own words, Gene recounts his 1988 hunt...

For 40 years, I have hunted cougar with hounds; and, hopefully, my 1988 hunt will not be my swan song. The last 30 years, I have hunted in the Selway Bitterroot Wilderness in Idaho each winter, trying to kill a Boone and Crockett record lion. Each winter for the last 20 years, I have hired a ski plane to fly me, my dogs, and camp, into the backcountry where I hunt for a month or longer. I prefer to start hunting about the first of February, as the weather tends to improve rather than deteriorate after that time.

That was my thought on February 3, 1988. The day dawned clear and cold, and since I had loaded my pickup the day before, all I had to do was to phone the local commercial fly-boy and make arrangements for the flight. I called Frank Hill, of Hill Aviation in nearby Grangeville, and told him I was ready to go.

After a 30-mile drive, I arrived at the airport around 9 A.M. and started loading my gear into a 180 Cessna ski plane. I'd done this many times, so I had a pretty good idea of what I was doing. When the load got to within a foot of the headliner, I stuffed my two hounds on top and we were ready for takeoff. The airstrip we were using was long and black, so there was no problem getting airborne. The strip we were going to, however, would be different.

Forty-five minutes later, and 100 miles east, we came to the snow-covered, 900-foot, private airstrip with a double dog-leg. Frank extended the skis below the tires and powered-in around the ridge to the final approach and we splashed down in 18 inches of fresh snow. My work was just beginning.

After unloading the plane, I packed all my gear 200 yards to the campsite. I had to clear snow for a place to set up my tent, then get the stove in place, and cut a good supply of wood. It was dark by the time I was finished, and the stars were out. The night was going to be really cold.

I'm 65 and have been a senior citizen for 10 years already. While I spend most of my life outdoors and take long summer and fall pack trips with my horses and mules, I wasn't ready to run up and down the mountains as I once did. Consequently, I spent the first week getting in condition and breaking the trails. The first three weeks, my dogs started and treed several lions, one of them a big tom and the rest females. None were big enough to consider taking. I was enjoying the action and the solitude.

Then came the morning of February 26th. It was clear and cold, and the snow was hard and crusted. After a good breakfast, I turned the hounds loose and headed for a saddle in a ridge a mile from the river. My dogs reached the saddle first and had a track started by the time I got there. But they'd trailed-off the other side of the ridge, down into the canyon, then up the other side and over the end of a ridge that came down from the high country. Not knowing if they were trailing forwards or backwards on the track, my only choice was to try to stay within hearing of them. In the steep Selway Bitterroot, that's not always easy. I headed up, staying on top of the ridge they'd crossed. From there, I could hear them well enough to know the direction they were going.

Three hours of uphill climbing later, I found where the dogs and lion had crossed the ridge that I was on. After another hour of steep climbing on snow that was getting soft, I could hear the dogs barking treed. They were still a long way off.

When I finally got to the scene, I found the cougar treed on a steep, north-facing hillside, in a tree that had fallen downhill and was not lying in the tops of others. When I saw it, I realized for the first time that my dogs had treed the cougar that I had spent most of 30 years looking for. It had been a long time since 1961, when the lion I killed that year had challenged Teddy Roosevelt's record cougar. I would take this cat.

The big lion was nervous and wanted to get out of the tree. I was nervous and didn't want him to jump. I had already gone farther down the mountain than I'd wanted, and I did not want him to jump and go even farther down into the canyon. It was already going to be a long trip out.

Light conditions for picture taking were very poor but I tried a few photos anyway, while the cat was still in the tree. Then I tied-up my dogs in case I had a cripple, a situation that can get dogs hurt or killed. The shots were at close range and the two slugs in the ribs from the .357 Mag (Model 19 Smith and Wesson pistol) put an end to the excitement.

Skinning the heavy cat on the steep hillside in two feet of snow was no small job. An hour later, I had his hide and head on my back and had started up the mountain. In another hour it was growing dusk and I was only on top of the first ridge. Camp was still miles and hours away.

I can only estimate the cat's live weight, but from experience and the size of the hide (laid-out on a log, it was 9 feet, 7 inches long) I'd put it at 225 pounds. While I would later find that the hide and head weighed 42 pounds and my backpack another 18 pounds making the entire load feel like it weighed 100.

It was dark when I hiked into camp three hours later and the stars were out again. It had been a long 27 years.

OFFICIAL MEASURER'S NOTE: What's there to say about this fine cougar trophy? At only 1/16 of an inch shorter in skull length than the current No. 1-ranked lion, there's very little room to argue that it's not a great, great cat! Interestingly, with the exception of a distinct outlier at 8-11/16 in skull width, Alford's cougar's 6-11/16 skull width is a mere 3/16 narrower than that of other top scorers on width.

Clancy the Caribou

Paul T. Deuling

Yukon Territory Mountain Caribou | Current Rank #1

P AUL T. DEULING HARVESTED HIS WORLD'S RECORD CARIBOU more than 20 years before he was able to participate in the Club's triennial awards celebrations. In 2010, he was honored at the Club's 27th Awards Banquet where he received the Sagamore Hill Award.

CIRCA **1988**

The Sagamore Hill Award was created in 1948 in memory of Theodore Roosevelt, Theodore Roosevelt, Jr., and Kermit Roosevelt to honor outstanding trophies worthy of great distinction. Deuling was only the 17th recipient of a Sagamore Hill Award.

Deuling received the award for taking a world's record mountain caribou in a hunt that exemplifies the sporting values that Roosevelt championed—fair chase, self reliance, perseverance, selective hunting, and mastery of challenges. The bull scores 459-3/8 points, more than 6 inches larger than the next-largest mountain caribou in Boone and Crockett Club's records book.

Deuling, who was 38 years old at the time, spotted the huge caribou during an August 1988 solo hunt for Dall's sheep in the Pelly Mountains of the Yukon Territory. The following is his own account of the hunt that was published several years ago in a book on Yukon hunts. One detail that Deuling is too modest to explain in the published story is that his hike into his hunting area was six miles. After he took his trophy it took five days, three round-trips—a total of 36 miles—to pack out his trophy and his camp.

In his own words, Paul recounts his hunt...

A lovely blonde lady from Vancouver who was visiting our family quizzically asked me, "Is that a very big moose you have on the wall there, Paul?" She had shown some interest in the taxidermy mounts in my basement as I had been explaining what the various animals were and generally where they were found in the Yukon. I replied that the animal she was referring to was a mountain caribou and that yes, it was a fairly large one.

"Oh," she replied, "does he have a name?"

This took me by surprise until she followed with, "I'm a vegetarian and the only way I can deal with seeing these animals is by giving them a name. His name is Clancy. Clancy the caribou."

And so it came to be that after all the years of roaming the Pelly Mountains and a few more years on my wall, Clancy finally received his name.

My hunt for Clancy was incidental to a Stone's sheep hunt that I had planned in late August of 1988 in the northern Pelly Mountains of the Yukon. All of my boys had either returned to school or hockey training camp so I decided to head out for a week's solitary Stone's sheep hunt before I, too, resumed my high school teaching duties. And I was frantic to go. That season had been a wet one and I had made several trips after sheep but either did not find them or sat in the tent for days before heading down the mountain for home.

With my old GMC 4x4 loaded down with my camper and extra gasoline, I headed for the Ketza country where I would have a walk of nearly a day before reaching my sheep area. The weather was absolutely beautiful with sunshine, a gentle breeze, and best of all, no bugs. Upon arriving that afternoon at my camp spot, a tiny sidehill bench, I kicked out a seat in the shale and chewed on some trail mix while watching a cow caribou in the basin below. She was foraging in the lichen, shaking her head and rubbing her back legs against one another in an effort, I supposed, to be rid of the bugs that were now appearing as the heat of the day dissipated. I watched her for a few minutes before she suddenly bolted off across the basin with head held high. And, just as caribou are apt to do, a few moments later she pranced right back to the origin of her fright. A wolverine was meandering in and out of the rocks and bushes, snooping into everything before loping off in his hunched-back fashion. The caribou was apparently fascinated by this, as she repeatedly ran off a short distance before turning, sniffing, and trotting right back to the disinterested mustelid, who just kept snooping for food. All this made great entertainment for a weary packer who was still sitting in sweat-soaked clothes and had yet to set up camp.

After pitching my tent, building a water pool from a tiny stream and setting out clothing to dry, I spent the next two hours having a snooze. Later that evening, I began to hike up the knob behind my camp where my boys had spotted rams on previous trips. Halfway up I remembered the silly cow and stopped to peer into the basin to see what she was up to. She had left the basin and climbed the very ridge I was on, but was grazing about 900 meters north of me. About 50 yards away from her was a large animal that appeared to have a black oak tree growing from his head. The huge bull caribou immediately grabbed my attention and I set up my scope to have a better look at him. After a quick calculation of the number of days I had to pack this guy out if I shot him, I decided that he was worth taking home. Big sheep could wait until next year.

The hike down to the tent became a scramble, as the closer I got to the tent and my rifle, the more excited I became. I had seen a lot of good bulls in the Pellys over the years, but nothing quite matched what this guy was wearing. A quick drop off for the scope and a snatch of the .270 sent me on my way down the ridge formulating a plan of approach as I crept between boulders. Dropping off the ridge and paralleling it seemed the sensible thing to do, and the stalk became much easier with a distinct dip in the topography ahead.

I was able to walk onto a ridge-cut that contained a pretty little tarn and then climbed about 40 feet to the rim where the bull was feeding. My last step was only enough to clear the ridge to allow viewing through my riflescope. Only 10 yards away, the large bull, resplendent in black velvet antlers and summer coat, could be heard munching as he tore up the lichen. I could see only a black mass through the scope, so I lowered it for a moment to assure myself that it was his shoulder that was filling up the aperture. At the shot, he bolted away and headed downhill toward the cow while I stood there dumbfounded that he would run at all. A second shot from 50 yards quickly brought him down.

I had not packed a camera since weight is an important factor in a solitary hunt, so I just sat beside the big fellow and stared at him. For how long, I don't know, but it was getting dark before I got around to caping and cleaning him. Few words can describe the feeling one has after killing such a magnificent animal, and I stopped many times just to stand back and view the scene.

The real work began the next morning when, loaded with meat, I began the first of three trips back to the truck. The loads were heavy, much heavier than I should have made them, but a 12-mile round trip up hills and over ridges is easier three times, rather than four. The next five days were spent pushing through willow brush and shin tangle with many a cuss word. "What a stupid, stupid thing to do!" was the most muttered phrase until I was done. However, the trip was worth the effort and my family dined on very tender caribou the following winter.

Tony Grabowski did a super taxidermy job on a shoulder mount and Clancy continues to impress hunters and non-hunters alike with his tremendous antlers.

And, from time to time, when the urbanites come to visit, I still hear, "that's a fine looking moose you have there!"

Reprinted with permission from Of Man and Beast, *an Amboca publication.*

Lady's Day in the High Country

Mavis M. Lorenz

Montana Bighorn | Current Rank #32

"**D**AMN, DAMN, DAMN. I SHOULD HAVE TAKEN THAT LEAD RAM of the five I saw opening day," I thought as I planned my next three days of hunting.

I saw 25 or so rams, with at least 12 of them presenting good shots, but they all appeared too young. I was warned by sheep-wise hunters, outfitters and game experts not to take the first ram I saw because they always look big to the novice hunter.

CIRCA 1993

I was a novice hunter, but I spent considerable time learning about bighorn sheep. I studied videos about sheep behavior and learned all I could about field judging of trophy bighorn rams. I read masters' theses from the University of Montana that reported the studies of bighorn sheep in my hunting permit district in Granite County, Montana. I picked the brains of as many knowledgeable people as would answer my questions. Still, I felt there was so much to learn in such a short time. *Would I find the ram I hoped to find? What if I didn't?*

After 18 years of unsuccessful attempts to draw a permit, this was my one and only chance. I would not be eligible to apply for another permit for seven years. By that time, I would be well over 70 and no longer able to climb mountains.

My plan for the next three days of hunting was to climb to my spike camp (a tiny mountain tent with backpacking equipment), hunt the benches on the northwest side of the mountain, drop into the next drainage, hunt out the pockets on a south-facing drainage, and on the third day, hunt down a long ridge back to the bottom.

I left the pickup in the dark and started climbing the 3,000 feet to the top of the mountain where I hoped to find sheep. I moved slowly and did a lot of looking and listening. I reached a point on the ridge at 9 A.M., set up my spotting scope and examined the edges of the openings above me.

I picked up four sheep in the scope. They were feeding away from me toward some benches near the top of the mountain. One ram looked like it deserved closer scrutiny. I decided to work my way up the mountain and position myself in order to locate the rams on the benches later in the day. I backed off the point and climbed up along a fringe of timber to a fallen fir free. The sun was starting to feel good, so I sat with my back against the downhill side of the log when I heard a rattle of balsam root leaves behind me.

"Nuts, here comes another hunter," I thought

Out of the corner of my eye I saw a ewe walking. It went around to the end of the log behind a Christmas tree-sized fir and stood 40 feet from me. It bleated softly and repeated it insistently. I heard the balsam leaves again. Mother ewe appeared and joined the first one. This was repeated and the pair became a trio. All this took place in a span of three or four minutes. The ewes nonchalantly moved across and down into some timber. They had no idea I was there.

I gave the ewes a half-hour to get out of the vicinity so I wouldn't spook them and started to put on my pack to move up the mountain. Just then, the five young rams trotted across the open hillside 150 yards above me. I waited for them to feed out of sight. Before they were gone, three more young rams appeared in the far corner of the hillside. I was surrounded by sheep. Every sheep in Montana's Rock Creek area seemed to feed between 10 A.M. and 1 P.M.

I waited another half-hour and worked my way up through a line of trees to the timber. A storm came in from the west so I hunkered down in a patch of young firs while the thunder grumbled. The rain didn't amount to much, so I decided to explore a few grassy benches toward the top of the mountain. As I worked my way through the benches, another storm cell came across the mountain. I decided to move to my spike camp before the storm hit.

I moved along too fast, not paying attention to my surroundings. Three magnificent rams stood up and stared at me from 40 to 50 yards. I had my hat in my left hand because I was hot and sweaty My rifle was in my right band. I remember thinking I didn't want to drop my hat for fear the sudden movement would spook the rams. The hat was still in my left hand as I brought my rifle up slowly and grasped the forearm. *Which of the rams was the biggest?* I couldn't tell. They weren't going to stand there much longer.

"Come on, Mavis. Put your research and experience to work. Make up your mind," I thought.

The middle ram turned and gave me a profile. That was it The ram's horns matched the criteria I studied on videos. The size of the hole in the curl, the drop of the bottom of the curl below the jaw line and the way it carried the mass of its base out to the fourth quarter told me this was a keeper. I didn't dare move into a kneeling position so I took an offhand shot. I was close and didn't want to shoot over the ram, so I held on its shoulder. I hardly remember squeezing the trigger.

KAPOW! Down went the ram I jacked in another cartridge, hit the safety, and climbed up to the ram. I hardly believed my eyes. The size of the ram looked huge with all those horns and large head.

"Yahoo! I did it! I did it!" I yelled. I was shaking as I cut out the month and date on my permit. I must have figured it three ways to confirm the date was October 6, 1993.

About the time I marked my permit all hell broke loose. The storm that had moved my way hit with thunder, lightning, snow, sleet and rain. The wind howled and the three snags overhead groaned.

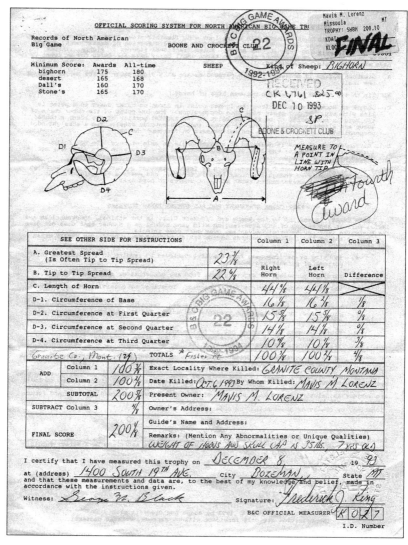

It was too dark to take pictures. I had to work quickly since it was almost 3 P.M. A taxidermist had shown me how to properly skin out the animal for a full mount. So, as the storm howled around me, I set to work. I had the ram skinned with the head and horns draped over a stump and the meat quartered in three hours.

Darkness was falling at 6 P.M. when I started down the mountain. I alerted a local outfitter that I had taken a ram and would need help in the morning hauling everything off the mountain. Rain poured all night and I didn't sleep much, worrying about the meat and cape. The ram wasn't disturbed when we returned the next morning. Four inches of fresh snow had fallen in my spike camp and rain and sleet made the day miserable, but I was so happy I hardly noticed. My feet were barely touching the ground.

After the 60-day drying period, my ram was scored by an official measurer for the Boone and Crockett Club at 200-1/8 points. Not bad for a woman who will never see 65 years of age again.

Trinity Dream Come True

J. Peter Morish

California Columbia Blacktail | Current Rank #7

THE VIEWS ARE BREATHTAKING, THE AIR IS CLEAN, AND THE hunting is exceptional. For 27 hunting seasons, I have experienced all that the Trinity Alps had to offer. For anyone who desires to hunt public land and wants a memorable hunting experience, the Trinity Alps may be their dream area; it has been for me.

CIRCA
2005

I have taken many deer in the Trinity Alps, both small and big. As the years passed, I became more specific on what size of deer I wanted to harvest. I found that passing up a legal buck was just as rewarding as taking a deer. When I got to the point of passing up a decent four-point buck to try for a larger one, then I knew that my perspective on hunting had changed. Most hunters in the United States don't associate good hunting with California, especially trophy deer hunting. However, I do.

The name Alps speaks for itself. Though the height of the Trinity Alps does not come near to the elevations found elsewhere, the steepness and ruggedness of the backcountry rivals the most well-known of tough hunting areas. Add to this the thick underbrush and you have a challenge for even the most seasoned hunter. The Columbia blacktail is certainly not as well known, or even hunted as much as the mule deer or the whitetail deer. However, it is every bit as much of a challenge and worthy adversary as any other species of deer. For many, the blacktail is one of the most difficult deer to hunt. To find a nice buck is a difficult and oftentimes daunting and consuming task. A trophy buck can require a lifetime of hunting. If you are able to hunt hard and choose to do so, then a trophy can be found in the coastal mountains of northern California.

As I have done for 26 prior seasons, I headed for my favorite hunting grounds in mid-September of the 2005 season. I often choose to not hunt the opening weekend because of the increased hunting pressure. After the opening weekend, the number of hunters in the backcountry drops significantly. Usually, the only hunters you see, if any, are those like yourself who have also hunted the area for years.

On this particular weekend, I planned on going with a hunting buddy but, at the last moment, he cancelled. Hunting in the wilderness is certainly not something I would recommend someone doing on his or her own. However, I had been planning this hunt since the end of the prior season, so I decided to go anyway.

The first leg of my hunting trip was to drive to the trailhead. I arrived early on a Friday morning. It was mid-September, which is often just an extension of summer. This day was clear, with temperatures in the low 90s. Though this area is known for hunters who horse pack into the wilderness area of the Trinity Alps, I had chosen to backpack. I did this because I have been able to do so physically and because I just didn't want those who would pack me in to know just how well I did hunting. It takes about seven hours of hard hiking to reach my camp. It is only about four or five miles, but the terrain is either up or down.

By the time I got to camp, I was extremely tired and sore. I was reminded of earlier hunts when it was difficult but not so consuming, and I wondered how much longer I would be able to do this kind of hunting. But, I was here now and tomorrow would begin another hunting season.

First, I needed to set up camp. When backpacking, you learn

to pack in only the essentials. If you do get a deer, then you will be packing out both the deer and all your gear. This can be a very heavy pack if you do not wisely choose what you bring. If I did get a deer, I would bone out the deer, cut the antlers off the head, and take the cape if the deer is a trophy animal. One of the positives of hunting the blacktail deer when backpacking is its size. It is smaller than mule deer or whitetail, so packing out the meat isn't too bad.

My camp was relatively simple. Over the years, I had cut out a level pad in a timber stand on the side of a mountain. This time of year the weather is often very nice, so a tent is not needed. I will lie out under the trees and peer through the tops to watch the stars. This is when I think about what tomorrow may hold and where I would hunt. The air was still and the skies were clear. Not the best conditions for hunting, but I was in the backcountry of the Trinity Alps and anything was possible.

The hunting area is so steep, rugged, and dense with brush that you just don't do any walking or stalking for deer. The area I wanted to hunt overlooks two ravines and a sidehill. It usually takes me about 30 minutes in the dark to find the rock outcropping where I would sit for the next three or so hours. From this place I would setup and spot for any deer that might be around.

I awoke well before dawn. I took my pack, which has an external frame. It comes in handy should I need to pack out a buck. I left for one of my favorite hunting sites.

I hiked out of the timber from camp and into a manzanita patch on the south side of the mountain. I snaked my way through brush and finally came to my rock. It was still dark and I had made little noise. I had made this trek from camp many times and I can do it in the dark with the help of a small flashlight, which I keep pointed on the path in front of me and toward the ground. I didn't want to alert the deer or other hunters that may be across the canyon. As I quietly set up on the rock, I began to see the faint light of the sunrise to the east. I could see the outline of part of the Alps. It was very quiet and still.

I use a lightweight eight power pair of binoculars and find that binoculars are the most important item in harvesting the deer other than my weapon. I began this morning by slowly working my binoculars across the hillside just adjacent and below me. With the binoculars, I continued to follow two ravines below the rock I was sitting on. I began to glass a second time, starting with an area directly across from me. I looked intently into an opening in the brush patch. The rays of sun were beginning to show over the mountains, but it was still relatively dark in the lower parts of the canyon.

I saw something across from me that looked out of place, but I couldn't see if it was a deer or just a shadow. I looked away and began to look lower on the hillside. It was still quiet and I hadn't heard or seen anything. I looked back at that spot adjacent to me and felt that something just wasn't right. I again looked intently, but I wasn't convinced that there was anything there. It was less than 100 yards away and I figured that I should be able to see a deer if it was there.

I looked downhill and then felt I needed to look back to that partial opening again. As I studied the area with my binoculars and as the light was getting better, I thought I saw what looked like a fork to a set of antlers. I just wasn't sure because there was so much brush in the area and things were not clear. As I was straining to see what was in the brush, I saw the entire top of the brush patch move slightly! I realized immediately that I had spotted a buck and the brush that moved was the deer's rack! I couldn't tell how many points it had but, as it moved, the rack looked to be the extensions of the brush patch that it was standing in front of.

I had seen and shot many big blacktails, but rarely had my heart begun to race at the sight of a deer. This was certainly the exception and my heart was pumping fast. It was now getting light enough that I could make out the outline of the deer's body. The deer was facing uphill and the front half of the body was behind a brush patch. Only his antlers from the middle of the ears up were visible above the brush. In the opening of the brush I could see from the middle of the deer's body to its back end. I immediately thought that all the buck had to do was take one step forward and he would be safe. From where he was standing, there was a steady and thick patch of brush running up the mountainside. If I was to get this deer, I was going to need some luck.

My gun was already positioned on the top of my pack on the rock. I quietly slid down onto my stomach and positioned the gun toward the deer. I located the deer in my scope, which I later determined to be 65 yards away, and to my surprise it was still standing in the same position. I could see him from midway back and felt this was going to be my only chance. Because of the size and number of points to the antlers, I was going to have to give it a try. I decided I had a pretty good chance of getting this buck if he would just stay still for another few seconds. If I could get a spine shot midway on the deer, it would be fatal. Being that the deer was as close as he was, I decided to take the shot. I lined up on the deer, held steady, and shot!

Through the scope, I saw the buck flinch and take a step backward. As I pulled away from the scope, I looked up to see the buck take another backward step and fall to the ground. He fell partially in the open in the brush, but only enough to see part of the body. He was down on his side and wasn't getting up.

It took a couple of minutes to compose myself and realize what had just happened. I knew I had just harvested a deer and he was huge, possibly the largest deer I had yet taken. It was still very early, so I decided to sit on the rock outcropping and relish the moment. I sat on that rock for an hour watching the sunrise and taking in the beauty that was revealed before me. The morning colors seemed brighter and the view even more majestic. I thought then that I probably had shot the deer of a lifetime. It had taken 27 years for my dream of a trophy to come true, but it happened and it occurred in the most beautiful area I have been fortunate enough to hunt — the Trinity Alps.

Out of Necessity

Sometimes there's no way around it—you have to hire a guide or hunt on private land. It may be that you don't have the proper backcountry gear, state game laws may require a guide, or it may be the only land available for the hunt. Nonetheless, great adventures can still be had!

Frederic Remington.

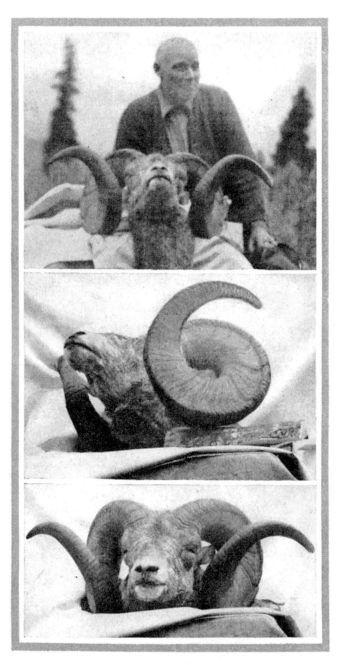

Three views of the record head, snapped in various positions to show the astonishing size of the horns. In the top view is the author in his hunting clothes

Record on a Meat Hunt

L.S. Chadwick, as told to Walter E. Burton

British Columbia Stone's Sheep | Current Rank #1

Editor's Note: Text and images from the February 1937 issue of Outdoor Life.

GOING OUT AFTER FOOD, AND COMING BACK WITH A SHEEP WHOSE horns measure nearly 52 inches along the outside curve may be something new in hunting, but that's the way I bagged the head that apparently sets a new world's record for size.

CIRCA 1936

The hunt really began 18 days before I shot the ram. I had decided to look for sheep in a wild section of the Rocky Mountains in British Columbia because, on a previous trip, one of my guides had told me that there were some excellent specimens in a small region apparently never hunted by a white man.

My party consisted of myself and three guides, Roy Hargreaves of Mount Robson, Walter "Curly" Cochrane of Rolla, and Frank Golata of Dawson Creek. Cochrane had operated a trap-line near the headwaters of the Muskwa River five years before, and had seen many fine heads. All of these men are good guides, excellent hunters and trappers, and experienced outfitters. It was due entirely to their abilities that I located, and got, the record head.

We went into the sheep country from Pousse Coupe, a place I selected because it had a good hotel where I could stay while getting my outfit adjusted for the trail. From there, we went to Dawson

Creek, seven miles farther up, and continued by automobile for 85 or 90 miles. We crossed the Peace River at Taylor Flats, and followed the river most of the time, going by way of Fort Saint John, to Bear Flats. There we picked up our pack train, and struck out into rough country. Going was often slow because, after leaving the regular beaten trails we had to blaze our own. Some days we made only six or eight miles. We pitched 16 camps in 18 days, having twice to remain an extra day in camp because of heavy rains. We left Bear Flats August 9, and worked our way northwest, up Halfway River, over the two Nelson Summits, past Redfern Lake, and then turned north. We fought mosquitoes and gnats all the way.

When we pitched camp on August 27, Curly, who at the time was acting as cook, demanded that some of us go out and get a supply of fresh meat. "We've been living on bacon long enough," he complained. And the rest of us agreed. When you eat bacon day after day for more than two weeks, you develop a craving for something fresher.

We had arrived at about 2:30 in the afternoon, so there was plenty of daylight left. Roy, Frank, and I took the glasses and rifles, and started out to scout. We decided that, although we were looking primarily for fresh meat, we would not shoot any sheep unless they had fairly good horns. Thus the scouting expedition had the double goal of food and trophies, but we never suspected that it would turn out the way it did.

Soon after leaving camp, we split up. Roy climbed to the highest point on a near-by mountain that faced our camp, and set the 20x telescope on its tripod. Through the 'scope, he searched the neighboring ranges for sheep. He saw about ten or a dozen rams, but none that seemed to have horns larger than 35 or 36 inches. Then, six or seven miles away, he located three sheep on the sky line of a high mountain range. "One of them looks as if it might be worth going after," he declared. Pursuit, though, was impossible in what remained of that day.

Early the next morning, however, we started after the three rams, hoping they had not strayed very far from the place where Roy had spotted them. We were optimistic, so we took horses to bring back the meat. About one o'clock, we stopped to eat lunch high up under a cliff, out of the wind. Not far away there was a high saddle of ground, near the top of the range. When lunch was over, we climbed to the saddle and surveyed the country with our glasses. We saw three sheep on top of a neighboring mountain, maybe a mile and a half away. One of the rams seemed to be carrying a wonderful pair of horns. We promptly decided to attempt a stalk.

The sheep apparently saw us. So Roy and I left the horses with Frank, who kept them out in the open where the sheep could watch them, and started after our game. We went down to the valley between the two ranges, along the edge of a glacier that partly filled a steep ravine, then crossed the valley, and scaled the other side. Of course, when we got to our goal the sheep were gone, but we soon sighted them in the next valley.

From this point, the biggest ram didn't look so promising. Roy and I debated whether to keep after him, or try to locate something better. We decided finally to keep on, now that we had gone this far, and get some pictures of him at least. Besides, we needed meat.

Aside from being a hunter who uses a gun, I also like to shoot wild game with a motion-picture camera, particularly game I am going to try to bag with a rifle. So we crept within 200 yards or so of the sheep, and I exposed some color film on him.

Finally, I decided to try a shot. I fired from a sitting position, and, as he was directly below me, and almost straight down, I aimed a bit low. I was using a telescope sight for the first time on game of any size. The bullet struck the ram low in the body without hitting any bones, and the ram left in a hurry. Roy and I took after him. All the sheep ran swiftly down the valley for a short distance, and then started to climb our side of the mountain. The wounded one soon began to lag behind, and, while he was running down the valley I took four more shots at him before he disappeared. One of the bullets struck him lightly in the hip. I shouted to Roy, who was able to make much faster time than I, to give him a finishing shot. I felt that the sheep was so badly wounded that he eventually would die, perhaps suffering for hours or days before he did.

Roy was fast outdistancing me in the chase. When a man gets to be 62, he has to move a little more leisurely than when he was young. I probably won't do much more hunting in a country where I have to climb mountain ranges 10,000 feet high.

The wounded ram was unable to keep up with the others on the upward climb allowing Roy to get near enough to get in the finishing shot. The bullet passed through the sheep's body, back of the shoulder and above my first one. The animal dropped down into a deep ravine. When we got to him, he was dead.

Even then we were not too enthusiastic about our prize, a Stone's ram (*Ovis stonei*). His body was small, at least for such a pair of horns. The big surprise came when we put the tape on him. The left horn measured 52-1/8 inches along the outside curve, and thirty-one and a quarter between the tips. The circumferences of the horns at the bases were a little more than 15 inches. We were so excited that we failed to notice then that a small portion of the point, perhaps 2-1/2 inches, was broken from the right-hand horn. Except for this, I am sure the right-hand horn would have been at least a half inch longer than the left, as it was larger at the base and throughout its length.

I remembered that the largest previous sheep head on record had horns measuring about 49-1/2 inches on the outside curve, so I obviously had the biggest wild-sheep head ever taken. Later checking showed that the finest sheep head of any species listed in *Records of North American Big Game* is that of the bighorn credited to James Simpson, who shot it in British Columbia in 1920. The horns had an outside curve of 49-4/8 inches and a spread of 23-7/8 inches. The largest Stone's sheep head, a trophy taken by C.R. Fahr on the Peace River in 1930, had a curve of 44-6/8 inches.

By the time Roy and I reached the dead sheep, Frank had become tired of waiting, and had started with the horses to follow us. Just as we were planning to go back and look for him, he appeared in the valley, scarcely 400 yards below. As he was able to lead the horses within 100 yards, we did not have to carry our meat very far.

We estimated, from rings on our ram's horns, that he was about 14 years old. He had excellent teeth, and otherwise was in good condition. All three of the men with me checked the horn measurements.

To my knowledge, Stone's sheep are found only north of the Peace River. There are no sheep of the common bighorn variety in that region. Stone's sheep are smaller body than regular bighorns and have very different markings. Whereas the bighorn has a white "doughnut" on its rump, the Stone's sheep has a white patch that extends all the way down to the ankles, like a pair of white pants. Its bluish-gray coat hasn't so much brown as the bighorn. The backs of the legs are white, the under body white or gray, and the fronts of the legs brown. Some specimens have white faces and necks.

Curly Cochrane told me there seemed to be only about one-fifth as many sheep in the territory near the headwaters of the Muskwa River as there had been five years before. Wolves, he said, were responsible. If something isn't done to clean out the wolves, it won't be many years until the sheep are extinct in that region. The wolves get them when snow drives them down into the valleys.

At a sulphur spring near where we camped, I shot a big male wolf, the leader of a pack of five. In every direction from that spring I found sheep horns, some of them very good. Such slaughter cannot help but thin out the sheep.

Chances of getting heads bigger than the one I took probably are none too good, for big heads are becoming scarce wherever hunters are active, because of the practice of shooting rams with horns no larger than 35 or 36 inches around the curves. Too many hunters shoot rams with small horns, and then wonder why no big trophies are left. The only reason I was able to get the big fellow in the Muskwa River country was that no other hunters had been through there to get him when he was smaller. He happened, too, to be lucky enough to escape the wolves. As we did not cover this entire section,

on account of heavy snow, there is a chance that some lucky hunter will some time find this old boy's daddy with a still larger head.

Most persons ask me what kind of rifle I use. My favorite for all types of big game hunting is a .404 Magnum, made by the late Frank Hoffman, of Cleveland. It shoots a 300-grain bullet at a muzzle velocity of 2,709 feet per second, and has about twice the power of a Springfield. With a heavier load, it is suitable for African game. There is no game in North America that it cannot kill with a 300-grain bullet. The gun weighs about 10 pounds.

My guide always carries my Model 54 .30-06 Winchester. In case anything happens to the big gun, the Winchester will then be on hand, ready for business.

I realize the magnum is a bit heavy for Rocky Mountain sheep, but I like its range, power, and accuracy. It has a remarkably flat trajectory. As for the range, a little experience I had with the second sheep I shot on my trip may illustrate that. I got within about 350 yards of him, and succeeded in taking some motion pictures through a telephoto lens. Roy suggested that, if I wanted that ram, I had better use the gun instead of the camera, because the sheep was moving away.

So I started shooting. I fired six shots, using iron sights but missed because the animal was far away and moving fast. Then I decided to try one shot with the 'scope sight, as I could no longer see him with the naked eye. We judged the animal to be a good half mile away, but the bullet struck him in the hip, and did plenty of damage. It was pure luck that I hit him, but the shot does illustrate the power of the magnum 300-grain bullet at such ranges. In the Stone's sheep country, it is difficult to get closer than 200 yards to one of the animals, because they have been made shy by constant attacks from wolves. So a gun with considerable hitting power and flat trajectory is necessary.

This second sheep, by the way, had horns measuring 42 inches around the curves, and thirty inches between the tips. It really was

Chadwick (left) with a timber wolf he shot on the hunting trip. Also pictured are his guides Roy Hargreaves and Curly Cochrane.

a much more beautiful specimen than the record one, and its horns were superior in color and general appearance.

I found plenty of other game north of Peace River, but used my movie camera more than my guns. In a basin on the south fork of the Muskwa River, we came upon a grizzly bear. I took movies of him, while he was stripping leaves from weeds and bushes, and eating them. Then I decided to try the rifle. I left the camera standing, and moved about 75 feet upstream, to be closer for the shot.

The first bullet struck the bear, and he came plunging down the little valley toward me. One of the guides decided to try his luck as a cameraman, so he aimed the moving-picture camera, and pressed the release. As the bear got fairly close to us, the camera developed a decided tendency to wobble. On the film, which we saw later, the image of the bear jumps wildly all over the scene. And the closer the bear gets to the guide, the more it jumps.

I finished the bear with a shot at close range, but the guide didn't know until afterwards that my gun had jammed because the follower plate had flipped over as I was loading by hand, and that the bolt of the rifle, which the other guide was getting ready to fire, had slipped out of the gun. If he had known, I don't suppose the bear would have stayed in the picture at all. Fortunately, I had shot grizzly before and was able to keep my feet on the ground while I got my rifle loaded.

I had planned to go about 100 miles farther north, but snow prevented it. However, I felt more than satisfied with the results of the trip. A number of other hunting expeditions into Alaska, Alberta, British Columbia, and Ontario had taught me that it is almost a rule that the prize trophy is taken on the very last day. The sensible thing to do, now that I had my trophy, was to quit, even if I had bagged it the first day with the first shot. The next time I hunt, it might not be a bad idea to go looking for meat instead of trophies.

Nearly 80 years ago, B&C Club Member James L. Clark put the last touches on the Chadwick ram housed at the American Museum of Natural History. Today, visitors to the Buffalo Bill Historical Center in Cody, Wyoming, will find this original trophy mount at the entrance to Boone and Crockett's National Collection.

Polar Bear Number 9

Robert B. Nancarrow

Northwest Territories Polar Bear | Current Rank #118

I HAD JUST BEEN THROWN FROM THE SLED, WHEN JOHN, MY GUIDE, prematurely threw out the anchor before the sled had slowed enough for a safe dismounting. I landed on my chest, with my rifle under me, sliding across the ice in the snow. We had tried to intercept a large boar that had been pursuing a sow, with two year-old cubs. We just weren't quick enough. The boar had reached the new ice, and was quickly on its way to the rough ice.

CIRCA
1997

Hunting polar bear by traditional means, using dog sled and Inuit guides, is without question one of North America's greatest challenges. We were using a team of seven dogs, solely for transportation. John didn't believe in chasing polar bear with dogs. His exact words were, "We will 'hunt' the polar bear with dogs." That's exactly what we were doing, the sixth day of my 15-day hunt.

At 180 yards, I quickly rested my .300 Winchester Magnum on the nearest block of ice, placed the crosshairs on the bear's shoulder, and pulled the trigger. At the report of the rifle, the bear stopped running and stood up. I was surprised I had not hit the bear, but now I had a standing shot. I squeezed the trigger a second time, again with no results. I shot a third, followed by a fourth and final shot, still with no results. I quickly checked my scope to see if it was loose, and inserted four more shells. By this time, the bear had started to run to the rough ice. I fired two more shots, making a total of six shots fired, and did not touch the bear. My guide looked at me with disbelief, but with calm reservations that we would see another bear and maybe get another shot. Not finding the scope loose, I blamed myself in my excitement for just plain poor shooting, never thinking that my gun was at fault.

That night it was very difficult to sleep, because I knew I had just lost a trophy of a lifetime. John was reassuring and I was able to finally fall asleep. The following day we started our hunt where we left off the day before. The tracks were still there, and the mistakes I made were still fresh in my mind. We then took to the huge track and started to hunt again. By noon, we came up against a wall of ice. John decided we would hunt in the direction of our main camp, 10 miles back. Not feeling as though I was going to have the good fortune of seeing a bear of that magnitude again, I sat in the dog sled with mixed emotions. John stopped and told me to stay with the sled as he climbed a large block of ice, to look for bear. He quickly motioned me to join him, and when I got there, he was pointing a quarter mile in the distance to a very large bear, eating a bearded seal. The bear was on new ice, approximately four to six inches thick. The wind was coming from the north, and was starting to pick up. According to our GPS, we were 22 miles west of Banks Island on the Arctic ice flows. I asked John if he would stay with the dogs, so they would not bark. I would make the stalk alone. He agreed and wished me luck.

I was now on my own, crawling the entire distance since there was nothing but smooth ice between me and the bear. On my belly, I was instantly aware that the ice was rolling under me. It seemed to intensify as the wind became stronger, but all that mattered was, I was getting closer to my trophy. I was now within 180 yards, and although my heart was hammering, I elected to take my shot from that distance. As I calmly squeezed the trigger, expecting to hit the bear, the horror of the day before became real once more. I fired the second, third and fourth shots, all with the same results. I could not hit the bear at this distance and had to come up with a different plan. My guide was too far away to get his rifle and the bear had now become nervous, moving further away. The one thing in my favor was the strong crosswind, and the constant cracking of the ice, which sounded as loud as the report of my rifle. The only two options I had were to give it up completely or get within bow range, and hope for the best. I chose the later.

I had waited for too many years, and spent more money than I could afford getting this far. Only a hunter could understand my decision. As I crawled to within 70 yards, I could truly see the bear's tremendous size. My heart was pounding out of control and I was actually starting to feel fear. At approximately 60 yards I decided to shoot, not knowing what to expect. As I pulled the trigger, I can honestly say I did not know what the results would be. I had the crosshairs on the shoulder of the huge bear, and the bullet struck three feet back from his front shoulder. The bear let loose a tremendous roar and started diagonally toward me. Seeing that the gun was that far off, I had to force myself to aim off the bear, in order to hit him again. It worked! The next bullet struck the bear in the chest. The bear turned sideways, going in the opposite direction, so I aimed at his hip, striking the bear square in the shoulder. I was out of bullets and the bear and I were now only 35 yards apart. The bear got up again. Knowing there was nothing I could do, I laid with my face on the ice, hoping he would not see me.

After what seemed like an eternity, the bear finally expired. By that time, I was so exhausted from fear, that I almost could not raise up to look at my monstrous trophy. We later discovered that my gun barrel was blocked with ice and had split at the magna-porting when I was thrown from the sled, causing its inaccuracy.

The bear was 10 feet, 9 inches from nose to tail, and was the ninth bear seen on my hunt—truly, the most fabulous creature I have ever seen.

My Last Bull

Duane R. Richardson

Arizona Bison | Current Rank #10

I WOKE UP MY SON, RUSS, THE MORNING AFTER HE HAD JUST PLAYED and come up short for the Arizona State Championships in football. I told him I had some good news and needed him to verify what I was looking at. He wandered in and looked at the computer screen in my office and confirmed my findings of having the number one of four bison tags for the House Rock Ranch hunt in northern Arizona. My excitement was shared by him and everyone else I could call at that early hour who might be interested in my glory.

CIRCA **2002**

My son wanted me to do the hunt with my bow. The tag allows you to hunt with any legal weapon, but I agreed with my son. My choice would be that of the stick and string.

Scouting started in January before the season to get the lay of the land, and possibly find a few big bulls in some out of the way places. The ranch manager stated that he had not seen nor heard of any bison since the first part of September. He also said that we would really have our work cut out for us.

That sentiment went right along with the videotape that the Game and Fish sends successful applicants. It basically says,

"Congratulations but get ready for the hardest hunt in the world."

I was never one to forego a challenge, so I put together a team of people who had expertise in each area needed. We were able to execute a wonderful game plan. I am blessed to have a family and group of friends who are without a doubt some of the best hunters in the entire west.

I would start my hunt in a very remote spot separated from the other hunters by many miles and an entire mountain range. I had the pleasure of meeting two of the other hunters on previous scouting trips, and they were really nice people who were going to be fun to hunt with. I told them of my plans to pursue with stick and string and they thought I was either crazy or just not really fond of bison steaks.

Orientation day arrived. Two weeks earlier, I had located in the area I wanted to hunt four bulls I believed would push the state record. After orientation, I drove back to camp in a blinding snowstorm that stopped around 3 A.M. "Perfect," I thought to myself.

We really needed to cover some ground and look for tracks in the area where I last saw the four bulls. At the end of day one, my dad, George, and Bill Bolt were able to come up with some signs we determined were three days old. Phil Dalrymple and I decided to track around and see what we could come up with on the next day. My uncle Bob and Craig Thornton would try to eliminate other areas where we might have missed the bulls from the day before.

Day two panned out nothing but cold, wet feet and sore leg muscles. Day three was pretty much the same thing. We would leave camp well before sunrise and return with headlights, covering literally hundreds of miles between us and not so much as a track found.

On day four, our excitement level soared to a new high. Phil had found some huge tracks leading east toward the plateau. I had already had visions of two huge bulls traveling together and just hanging out away from the rest of the herd. The further we tracked, the deeper the snow got, to the point where we guessed it to be 36-inches deep. We finally reached the time of day where we were running out of light and the tracks were still heading up the plateau. We decided to back off and come back the next morning.

While en route to where we had cut tracks the day before, we cut one single set of tracks headed out of the deep snow to the west. We tracked them over 10 miles, taking up most of the day, only to find they belonged to the biggest bull I had ever seen! The problem was the bull was a stray cow from a cattle herd. The tracks of a cow and a bison are identical, and cannot be told apart by even the most seasoned hunter or rancher. However, after day five it was pretty depressing to say the least.

We determined that we needed to change location, and day six was spent moving the camp a hundred miles away, closer to the House Rock Ranch. Arriving at the ranch, we learned that two of the four hunters were finished. One hunter remained and had taken his horses back to Phoenix for some fresh stock.

Several years ago, the first archery bison hunt on the north Kaibab was undertaken by my father. He was able to connect on a bull the first day of a 30-day hunt. Dad's experiences on the Kaibab for those many years were invaluable when it came to planning the rest of our hunt. There was an area above the ranch that we knew would hold some big bulls. We spent the afternoon of the seventh day trying to figure out a way to access that area. Phil had some commitments he needed to get back for, so he left around noon.

While looking for an access point across a huge canyon, my dad, Craig, and I came across two very large sets of tracks. Dad was elated at the freshness and size of the tracks. He told me, "Corky, this is a huge bison."

I remember telling him (after spending day five tracking down a cow), "No, Dad, those are just rogue cattle."

He answered back, "If these are rogue cattle, then they are carrying around bison hair and fur with 'em because I found enough to stuff a volleyball with."

He was right! After seven days, we finally had a track that was under two days old. I grabbed my pack, bow, and quiver and began

tracking. The bison seemed to be spending most of their time in an open field that provided good feed. I cut some tracks that had very sharp edges on them. They had to have been made that morning. The bison chips were extremely fresh. The tracks headed down a pinyon-juniper point that is half a mile long and half a mile wide—a good bedding area, heavy with shade.

A light snow had fallen and I decided to check around the bedding area to see if I could find tracks leading out. I made a circle around the point without finding any tracks leading out. It was around 4 P.M., so I decided to start at the end of the point and work my way back to the feeding fields to the west. Four hundred yards into the point, I found two fresh beds still warm. What really got me excited and had me nock an arrow on my string was when I found foamy urine with the bubbles popping on a flat rock.

The wind was perfect, blowing from west to east as I entered the feeding area. All of a sudden, the ground began to shake as two bulls came running from the south and headed toward a small draw. What went wrong? The wind was perfect, and I knew they had not heard me. Something or someone had spooked them.

After spending seven days looking for the quarry, I was just thankful and praising God that I had seen bison—running or not. I hurried over to the edge of the draw where they had disappeared, only to find the biggest one had stopped across a small draw. I remembered thinking to myself, "If that bull would just turn and come back to the feeding grounds, I will be in good shape."

As if on cue, the bull—seemingly not knowing what had spooked it—turned and headed back uphill to the west of me. I hurriedly took off my boots to do the shoeless dance one more time. I ran 200 yards while quartering towards the bull in order to get a lane where I could get a good shot.

The bull stopped in an opening 35 yards away, with only its head entering the opening. I could see its right side and knew it was something special. If it would only stop for a minute to give me a good shot. I was already at full draw for about 15 seconds, waiting for it to move. The bull finally stepped forward and I released the arrow. The arrow got there faster than I anticipated. I hit it square in the front shoulder, just up from the leg.

I immediately grabbed another arrow and ran up the hill to cut the bull off in order to get another shot at it. I was uncertain how much penetration I had made from my first arrow. To my amazement, the bull had already begun to weave and was having a hard time standing up. The arrow had penetrated to the opposite shoulder and only my fletch remained visible.

I followed it about 150 yards before it stopped for the first time. This time the arrow penetrated dead middle and dead center. The bull walked away and I pursued it, grabbing for arrow number three.

While in pursuit I was locked in and focused on getting shot three away. Then I heard a sound. "Psst."

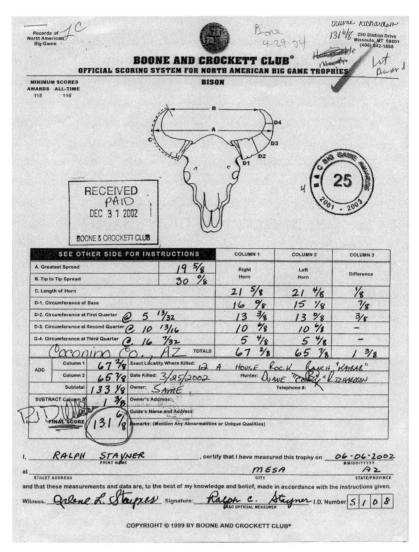

"Psst," I think I heard something again.

"Corky," I hear, in a loud whisper. Standing on a small rim, above where the bull had just stopped, stood Dad and Craig. They went on to tell me how they had found these two bulls in the feeding area that they had spooked after catching sight of them. They felt about as high as a wart on a snakes belly after running off the only two bulls we had seen in a seven day period, especially without being able to find me. They explained that they were just following the tracks where the buffalo had spooked, when all of the sudden, they saw the largest of the two coming toward them. Unbeknownst to me, the bull had stopped no further than 10 yards below them. My dad was wondering where I was, when all of the sudden he heard the sound of an arrow. The next thing he saw was an arrow sticking out of the bull in the ten-zone. He kept telling me that I needed to slow down on my pursuit, but the view he had of the bison was of its left side and he didn't know that I had a well-placed arrow on the right side. The bull went down no more than 75 yards from our conversation.

Kaibab is laced with wilderness area from one end to the other, but this bison chose to die on a two-track logging road. Packing would not be a problem. Once we approached the bison, my dad knew right away that he had never seen a picture nor heard of one with this size of horns. The bull expired with one side of the horn down in the dirt, and it took all three of us to turn its head around and see if we had two sides that matched. Indeed we did!

I was able to get a hold of Phil before he had made his trip back to Tucson. He had traveled halfway when he heard part of a broken-up cell phone message from me. He determined that one of two things had happened: either I needed help or I had gotten a bison. Either way, he was headed back. He found us around midnight.

I drove down to the game manager's house to get him to confirm a bow kill before any field-dressing took place. He couldn't believe that I had actually killed one with a bow on one of Arizona's most difficult hunts. When he saw the bison, he said that to his knowledge, he had not seen that particular bull. He aged the bull according to the jaw age charts at over 16 years.

God had blessed me way beyond my wildest dreams with an exceptional animal and extraordinary friends and family that will remain with me for a lifetime and an eternity. Did I mention that he died on an old road? If you have ever skinned and quartered a 2,000-pound animal then you know how truly blessed I was.

A Stone for the Ages

R. Terrell McCombs

British Columbia Stone's Sheep | Current Rank #71

S HEEP HAVE ALWAYS HELD A SPECIAL FASCINATION FOR ME. MAYBE it's because they live in such spectacular, harsh environments. Maybe it's because they represent such a tremendous physical and mental challenge. However, I think the real basis for my fascination is simple: It's those horns! I don't know many hunters who aren't in awe of holding a really good set of heavy, massive sheep horns in their hands.

CIRCA
2007

It was in September 2007 that I set out to find a Stone's ram to add to a fine Dall's ram I had harvested in Alaska's Chugach range. That was in 2004, and although I hunted these "rams of the rocks" in 2006, I had been unsuccessful. Now at 52, I can see the horizon of my sheep-hunting career much clearer than I could a decade earlier. We only have so much time to do what we love, and I was determined to take a good Stone's ram, arguably one of the most beautiful and coveted big-game animals in North America.

The final floatplane ride into Jerry Geraci's Stikine River Lodge was smooth and the scenery spectacular. After touching down, I ate a fine meal of sheep ribs prepared by Ruth, the lodge's cook, and sacked out for a good night's rest. The following morning would find me in the saddle for a 25-mile horseback ride with a pack string into some of the wildest country in North America.

My guide was Rod, a 33-year-old fireman and mountaineer from Vancouver, British Columbia. Rod enjoyed taking a month's vacation every year to guide for Jerry. He was athletic, offered intelligent conversation on a wide variety of subjects, and was well-versed in sheep behavior and ecology. While Rod had guided many hunters to moose, caribou, goat, and even grizzly, he freely admitted that this was his first opportunity to guide a sheep hunter. Normally this would concern me, but not with Rod. While I have a decent amount of sheep- and goat-hunting experience, his attitude and confidence was infectious.

He said, "Terrell, all you and I have to worry about is the weather. We'll find a ram because I saw a real good one up here last week when I was glassing for moose down in the valley."

"How good was he?" I asked.

"Oh," Rod replied, "He was good al' right. It looked to me like his horns came two or three inches above the bridge of his nose and he looked plenty heavy."

He curled above the bridge of his nose? What a ram! I thought. Now I was excited and in the game. Later that evening we arrived at our campsite, and I stole some time to glass for sheep while helping set up camp. Nothing motivates a sheep hunter like sighting a big ram.

The next morning Rod and I left Earl, our young wrangler, in camp as we backpacked two or three miles to a good spike camp location to glass for the ram. We hunted and glassed hard for nearly three days, climbing up to look over several basins and an untold number of shale slides. No sheep. The fourth and final day found us tent-bound as the weather cooled considerably and six inches of snow greeted us at dawn. It snowed all day.

When you are 6-foot, 5-inches tall, spending the day cramped into a small backpack tent with your guide is a challenge to your commitment. Little doubts and questions enter your mind as to why you are really there. It also offers you too much time to think about your responsibilities back home. I tried to keep my mind busy by reading or simply sleeping. Bad weather is the curse of sheep hunting.

I have always thought the greatest challenge with hunting sheep is the mental aspect of it. You begin asking yourself too many questions when you are confined by the weather. *How many days are left? Will I find a good ram? Will the weather ever clear up? Will that head cold turn into something worse? What if the shot is too far? How's my family?* That is why I'll glass and trek to the top of every visible mountain before I'll spend one daylight hour in a tent. The problem is you never have any choice in the matter. Weather dictates everything. If you don't have the visibility to glass, you can't hunt sheep.

We glassed for an hour the next morning before bad weather descended upon us again. All we saw was one lone billy goat, but no sheep. At that point we decided to return to Earl and the horses. We at least had a larger tent there. We approached camp and called out for Earl around mid-morning. The 18-year-old was ecstatic to see us. I don't think Earl enjoyed those lonely days by himself! However, he offered good news. He had been riding up to a nearby pass early that morning and had seen a good ram feeding. We excitedly asked him for more details. After listening to Earl and asking several questions about the animal, Rod concluded that it was the same ram we had been looking for. The weather was clearing some, and we decided look for the ram that afternoon.

We hunted very hard, glassing into high mountain basins, while sitting out wave after wave of snow and sleet descending upon us from the northwest. It was strange. There were periods you could see a mile or more, closely followed by periods where you could not see 100 yards, coupled with high winds. We stuck it out all afternoon in search of the ram. We glassed and hunted over the high mountain pass and the adjoining mountains and deep cirques for nearly seven hours. Only the approaching dusk pushed us back toward camp. While the scenic vistas had been beautiful, we hadn't seen any sheep.

That evening, a serious storm blew in, dumping more than a foot of snow on top of an already hefty accumulation. The temperature dropped into the high teens and the next day was spent in the tent. No one, as I mentioned earlier, likes being confined to a tent because of weather. The time passes slowly and cabin fever can build up in hunters and guides alike. Earl and Rod were singing the blues that evening. Now, with only two full days left to hunt, the warm fires of Jerry's Stikine River Lodge were becoming more and more appealing. In fact, the idea of heading back early was even mentioned. I can't blame the guys. We were all a little down over the weather. That's when I reminded them to maintain a positive attitude.

I said, "Many great animals have been taken on the last hour of the last day of the hunt. We are going to tough this thing out. Who knows? The weather could clear up tomorrow and we could climb up to that pass and take the ram of the century."

I had no idea how prophetic those words would become.

The next morning dawned with fog, snow, and a gray overcast but there was a hint of blue in the western sky. Sure enough, it cleared enough by 11 A.M. to hunt. We busily packed our gear and began climbing toward the pass.

The going was slow as we pushed through snow two to three feet deep. I was in the lead and stopped to glass often. After an hour, we were a little more than halfway to the head of the pass when I noticed something unusual about 1,200 yards away on a south facing slope. Any big-game hunter knows what I am talking about. It just looked out of place. Slowly and quietly I held up my hand to stop our progress. I pointed toward the slope, and three pairs of binoculars went up at once. My breathing stopped for a moment as I realized I was looking at a very good bedded Stone's ram. He had not seen us and we slowly dropped out of sight into a side canyon.

I can't exactly describe the next few moments except to say the debate over stalking strategy was heated and intense. Finally, Rod and I agreed on the most conservative approach to the ram. After my disappointing experience the prior year, I had developed a deep respect for the powerful vision of these animals. I would not make the same mistake twice.

We lunged through the deep snowdrifts, my lungs burning as we pushed up an adjacent slope to reach a good shooting position. Although we were only at a little over 6,000 feet, the steep slope and deep snow made every step feel like 30-pound weights were strapped to each leg. Earl was paralleling us, peeking around the edge from time to time to keep an eye on the ram as we ascended. Suddenly, he motioned that the ram was up. He could not have seen, heard, or smelled us. Regardless, he was headed straight up the slope toward the crest of the adjoining drainage. We shifted into high gear as we cursed the snow and the icy mountain as we slipped and struggled the last 50 yards to the crest.

I had wanted a shot under 300 yards, but there was no hope for that now. I flopped down into the snow and grabbed Rod's pack for a rest. I was still heaving from the hard climb and took several deep breaths to calm my nerves as I tried to prepare for the shot of my life. I settled down as the ram continued toward the crest of the ridge, now less than 25 yards away. He was moving with purpose and there would be no way to keep up with him under these conditions. It was now or never.

"Earl, give me the range."

"476 yards," he replied.

Rod urged me to hurry before the ram disappeared over the ridge. However, I ignored his urgings, as I concentrated fully on the shot. It was still and silent, nearly solemn, like being in a cathedral. I was in a deep zone of concentration now, and my world went into slow motion. I took two more slow, deep breaths and acquired a solid, steady sight picture. Earl was saying something to me, but I didn't hear him. Every ounce of concentration was on the ram. I slowly began my trigger squeeze and I remember being surprised as the loud report of the rifle disturbed the deep stillness of the wilderness.

I saw the ram fall as I recovered from the recoil. I was turning toward Earl, with a look of triumph on my face, when he screamed, "You killed him!"

Earl, his face showing a combination of shock and elation,

leaped on me, driving us both down into three feet of snow. It was an act of pure joy. Suddenly, Rod joined the dog pile and the three of us laughed and shouted in victory as we rolled through the deep snow like schoolboys on winter vacation. We had been three men, thrown together as strangers in the intense crucible that is sheep hunting. Now we were laughing, screaming, and even shedding some tears in pure celebration of the hunt. It was a scene as old as mankind itself, and we continued to hug and shake hands, delirious over our success. We thought we might be shut out, but in the last inning, grasped victory! It is a feeling I cannot explain, but will never forget as long as I live.

We approached the ram together, for through this bonding experience we were now a team. I pulled the trigger but each of us owned a piece of that ram. No one had to say anything. We all knew it. I observed that his bases looked larger than 13 or even 14 inches. A tape measure was back at camp, but we weren't too concerned about it. We were just thrilled to have harvested such a fine animal. After plenty of pictures, we began the long pack down to camp.

I took out a vinyl tape measure in camp and casually measured the horns, mostly out of curiosity. The tape said 43 x 15 inches. Earl, ever the skeptic, insisted we measure them again. The results were the same. His horns didn't look that long due to their heavy mass. No one said anything for a few minutes as we began to realize the true size of this magnificent animal before us. I told Rod it was a heck of a way to begin his sheep guiding career and then kidded him that it would be all downhill from here.

Later, Jerry said it was the largest ram to come out of his area in nearly 25 years. No one had seen him before, strong testament to the fact that it is very hard to hunt every inch of a 4,000-square-mile hunting concession, even over 25 years. We carefully green-scored him at around 180 points. Roger Britton, the government inspector and a local taxidermist in Smithers, said it was the largest ram he had seen in more than 20 years on the job. He aged the ram at 13-1/2 years old.

Large rams are where you find them. I have heard it said that all the great Stone's sheep were taken in the 60s and 70s and none are left in British Columbia and the Yukon today. Great sheep are still there and more probably die from worn teeth and wolves than most of us would care to admit. However, with recent commodity prices at historic highs, more resident hunting pressure is put on sheep today than in the past. Once-formidable wilderness is being carved up and penetrated with easily accessed mining roads. High prices, due to the world's growing demand for energy and minerals, are a fact of life today. No outfitter can control that fact; he can only work to gain the cooperation of these natural resource companies in order to respect the wildlife that is his living. Let us hope this sense of cooperation in land-use management is successful. It is important because today more than ever, we need to know that great rams still roam wild in steep mountain basins.

Fortunately, this hunt proved to me they still do.

We Got a Stomper!

Rip Rippentrop

Montana Bighorn Sheep | Current Rank #9

THE LAST THING I SAID TO MY FRIEND JOHN WILDEBOER AFTER he harvested his great 2005 South Dakota Black Hills ram was, "Before I die I will go on my own bighorn sheep hunt." Who knew that five years later I would draw the Holy Grail of all sheep hunts in the beautiful Missouri River Breaks of Montana. The research began immediately and lasted for the duration of the summer. I was determined to make the best of the opportunity I was given with the seven weeks of vacation I had available to use.

CIRCA
2010

There were many sleepless nights throughout the summer in anticipation of the hunt. In July, my dad and I took our first scouting trip from South Dakota to the Breaks. We did not see any sheep on the north side of the Missouri River, but we did see 20 rams on the south side, and one was a monster. In August, Tom Powell and I went for a three-day scouting trip to the areas we wanted to concentrate on for the upcoming hunt.

Finally, the archery season arrived! Jared Bouman, Tate Bouman, and I arrived in the Breaks September 2 to do some scouting before the archery season opened on September 5. We saw about 10 rams, and 2 were in the 180-class. Rattlesnakes were a constant concern, because they were seen and heard daily. Chance Wooden Knife—Game, Fish & Parks Director for the Rosebud Sioux Tribe—came up for the next six days. We packed in three miles through a couple deep coulees and camped for three nights. We found another 10 rams and three 180s.

My dad came up for the next six days, and we started hunting a new area—not one ram was found for three days. For the opening day of rifle season, we decided to go back to where we started. On September 15, we spotted our first 190-inch ram. He was bedded down, but the following morning he went onto private land. With weather moving in and Dad having to head home, we pulled out at noon. The next day, I got a phone call from another hunter who said, "Rip, I wanted to make you feel good about leaving. It was a downpour that turned into snow by morning. You are lucky you got out of here." When it rains in the Breaks, you usually can't get around for a day or two. Regardless of the weather, some great rams were harvested during opening week of rifle season and I was second-guessing myself for leaving.

I knew we would not be going back to the Breaks for nearly 45 days until the rut started in November. I called some of my sheep hunting friends from Wyoming, Brian "Hip" Moore, Larry Brandt, Buck Porter, and Chuck Woodman—I called them the Wyoming Sheep-Wrecking Posse—to meet up at the Breaks. We all got there on November 1 and set up our wall tent at a local rancher's place for our base camp. Hip told us all that first night, "We need to find a Stomper!"

Over the next few days, the weather was great and everybody was in awe of how many book rams we spotted. You have to see it to believe the quality of the rams in the Breaks. Josh Keller also showed up for three days to help with the glassing efforts. The following days we saw three 195-inch rams that we called Dino, Grand Daddy, and Lunch. Wow, were the guys upset with me for deciding not to pursue any of these three rams! I kept telling them my goal was a 200-inch ram, and I had the whole month of November off for vacation. At camp that night, we discussed how we felt like we were chasing a ghost, and I said, "Our day will come, guys. Everything will click, the stars will align, and the Big Guy in the Sky will shine down on us."

On November 6, it was just Hip and me left to hunt, and we were prepared to stay until the season closed on November 28.

The next day brought a heavy rain—the low point of the hunt. During the rain/sleet/snow storm, the temperatures dropped from 70 degrees to 10 degrees that day, and the sheep patterns completely changed. That night Hip and I went into Winifred, Montana, to get our first shower in eight days, eat a cheeseburger instead of a can of chili or MREs, and to make some phone calls.

I called my wife Chidawn to let her know we hit rock bottom with the weather and felt we needed to try to find Dino again. Her reaction was, "What the heck!" I asked her what the problem was and she said, "There's a problem with you! I'm mad! You are not going to shoot a 195-inch ram with all the effort you have put in all summer and the vacation you have left to use! I'm going to hang up on you after I tell you this, don't come home unless you shoot a 200-inch ram!"

Hip said, "I guess we're not shooting Dino and we do have 21 days left to hunt, bud. Back to work, Rip!" Man, was that the shot in the arm we needed.

The next morning Dad was back in camp for four days, and we were back to the drawing board. The last day Dad was there, Larry came back to help for the next three days. That night, I had great news for everybody! After splitting up for the last few days, I had found a big ram in a new area, and we needed to take a closer look at him. I hated to see Dad leave and not be around for the big day, but he had pheasant hunting in South Dakota on his mind. We did find the big ram the next day—I named him Money—and thought he might reach the 200-mark, but there was one problem. He was on private land that we did not have permission to hunt. There we sat for three days, watching the Money ram from a mile away, waiting for him to come

Rip, second from left, with his "Wyoming Sheep Wrecking Posse"
from left: Larry Brandt, Chuck Woodman, Buck Porter, and
Brian "Hip" Moore.

to us. Larry had to leave and we still had 14 days of hunting left, but that evening we saw another ram come marching into the band of ewes with the Money ram. Hip immediately said, "Rip, you better take a look at this ram!" At first I was cautious to agree he was bigger, but once they were both standing side-by-side rubbing their horns on the same sagebrush, there was no comparison between the two of them.

The next morning we went to Winifred to have Nick Econom look at the pictures we had taken of both rams. Nick said smiling, "Rip, this ram is going to surprise you and it's going to be in a good way!" The phone call then went to Bill and Renita Brown with Chase Hill Outfitters who uses Jon Barker Trophy Hunts for bighorn sheep hunts. After talking with Bill, he gave us permission to go after the new ram on his land without being guided. Once there, we got out of the pickup and as I leaned down to take my spotting scope out of my pack, Hip whispered, "Rip, your last star just aligned, and he is walking over the hill!"

I looked up, and sure enough it was the new ram walking toward us at 250 yards. I asked Hip, "Are you sure he is a 200-inch ram like we think?"

He said, "He's the biggest ram we've seen!"

After our discussion, and with sheep fever setting in, I harvested my ram at 230 yards. As he ran down a deep coulee, I realized the hunt had come to an end.

The next thing I remember, I was standing over the top of my blonde-haired ram with my eyes closed. Thanking the ram, the sheep gods, and the big guy in the sky. Hip walked up and said, "What do you think buddy?"

I said, "I don't know, I haven't opened my eyes yet. Is he as big as we thought?"

Hip said, "We got a Stomper! Open your eyes buddy!" We were both in awe of finding the 200-inch ghost. After celebrating and taking pictures, it took five hours to cape and pack the dark-horned ram out with our extra packer Brady Martin.

That evening we rough-taped him at 205-6/8 inches, concluding 38 unbelievable days in the Breaks. We then checked the ram in with Montana Fish, Wildlife & Parks (FWP) and were off to Cody, Wyoming, to Dewey's Wildlife Studio. After 60 days of drying, the ram was officially B&C scored by Fred King at 203-6/8 inches, with bases of 17-4/8 inches and 17-2/8 inches, and curls measuring 43-3/8 inches and 40-5/8 inches.

I would like to thank the big guy in the sky, my hunting partners, all the ranchers that allowed me hunt, the 150 people who took a phone call from me, the town of Winifred for treating us like one of their own, Montana FWP, and my company, Banner Associates, for allowing me time off to chase bighorn sheep. This hunt took a lot of teamwork, but I could not have done it without 100 percent support from my wife, our five kids, and my parents. Thanks for letting me live the dream!

When the Smoke Cleared

Thomas L. Mello

California Tule Elk | Current Rank #21

IN MID-JUNE 2011, I RECEIVED MY LONG-AWAITED DRAW RESULTS and was ecstatic to learn that I had been drawn for bull elk in Stonyford, California. Elk tags are very hard to come by in California, and tule elk tags are even rarer. I drew one of only two permits for this unit. I had been watching these elk since I was a kid, and the California Department of Fish and Wildlife had only recently opened a muzzleloader season on them.

CIRCA *2011*

Shortly after I received confirmation of my draw, I enlisted the help of a local rancher and guide, Pat Callahann, who is from Stonyford. Pat has extensive knowledge of the elk and the surrounding area.

I also started going on scouting trips with my wife Danyelle and my two sons, Thomas, 3, and Drake, 2, to the backside of East Park Reservoir, which is located near Stonyford, a small ranching community nestled in the foothills and valleys on the far west side of northern Sacramento Valley.

In the beginning, we saw very few elk on the public hunting area, while we were seeing big bachelor herds on the private ranches. However, the elk we saw in our hunting area were cows and calves, which the locals said would bring the bulls in when the rut began. We spent six weeks watching and patterning these magnificent animals, and we fell in and out of love with different bulls as more and more began to crawl out of the woodwork.

In between scouting trips, I began to work on my black-powder shooting skills. As a complete novice to this craft, it came with a much larger learning curve than I had expected. In the beginning, I was unable to shoot groups at 50 yards, and at one point I wondered aloud, "What have I gotten myself into?" But with increased practice and tweaking of loads, I was soon able to shoot a 2-inch group at a hundred yards, which by normal standards is poor, but I felt pretty comfortable with my new skills.

Three weeks before the hunt, the first bulls began to show up at the Bureau of Land Management property on the lake, and we became very excited. This was mid-August and the temperature was well over 100°F.

The public hunting area is located on the southwest corner of East Park Reservoir. The terrain consists mostly of rolling hills and small finger canyons with patches of thick valley oaks intermixed with wild oats and native grasses. In the spring, these hills are breathtakingly green and covered with wildflowers. By mid-August, however, they are reduced to nothing but knee-high, dried brown grasses gone to seed.

Most of the small canyons run east and west and drop gradually into the backwaters of the lake. These pockets were in stark contrast to the dry, arid hills above. They were lush and green, filled with cool water. These fertile waters teemed with life below the surface; largemouth bass, crappie, and bluegill could be seen feeding and finning, as well as an occasional carp slurping his way across the surface. Above, bullfrogs serenaded the mallards, wood ducks, and blue herons.

As soon as the sun ducked behind the western mountains, the hills came alive with pre-rutting elk, and small bands of cows, calves, and bachelor bulls emerged from all the fingerling canyons.

They stampeded their way to the waterholes to cool off and socialize. Many times in our scouting trips I counted over a hundred head of elk. It was incredible. From our vantage point under a giant white oak tree, we would often see Columbia blacktail deer, valley quail, red fox, gray fox, and coyotes. Watching them helped us pass the time until the magic hour when the elk arrived at the waterholes.

Two weeks prior to the season, I called and spoke with the biologist for a mandatory hunter session in which he explained how the hunt worked, the boundaries, and also explained a change in the rules. They had terminated the early and late bull hunts, and replaced them with a single bull hunt during which both bull tag holders for this unit could hunt at the same time. This worried me because it is only a 2,000-acre parcel to hunt, and while that sounds like a large piece of ground, I was worried that if the elk were spooked, they would flee onto private land where access is either not available or is very expensive. Furthermore, while there were a lot of big bulls milling around, one bull in particular in the herd had clearly established himself to be head and shoulders above the rest. I thought, *two hunters, one big bull...this could get tricky!*

The night before the season, I sat at my usual spot with my wife, the boys, and my guide Pat. We watched the elk filter towards the refreshing water. By now they had split the cows into small harems. The bull I wanted controlled the lion's share of the cows and the waterhole we had been watching. No other bull even attempted to challenge him.

Small satellite bulls bugled from under the shade of oak trees, taunting this brute, but stayed well out of reach of his antlers. We watched these guys bed down and walked out in the dark, anxious for what the next day would bring. We formulated a plan to sneak in under cover of darkness. We figured we would be able to get within 70 yards of where the bull was and take care of business at first light.

When we reached the parking area, I was surprised that the other hunter was not there camping or scouting. I had heard through the grapevine that he had another out-of-state elk tag and would not be coming until the latter part of the week. I was secretly relieved when he was not there.

That sleepless night was spent five miles down the road at Pat's house. At 2:30 A.M., we could not take it anymore: Pat and I left his ranch to go watch the sunrise at the lake. When we arrived at the parking area, the other hunter and his friend had arrived and were asleep in a make-shift camp. We spoke briefly and exchanged pleasantries and left quickly to get in position.

The night was warm, still, and quiet; the moon was three-quarters full. It seemed like forever, but as dusk turned to dawn, I heard the voices of the other two hunters coming down the canyon towards us. We were dug-in pretty good, so they were startled when we greeted them. They were apologetic and agreed to pull back and hunt a different area, but I could see the disappointment in their faces. They pulled back a few hundred yards and then dropped down and undercut our position. In doing so, they had the wind at their back blowing down over the waterhole.

When it was light enough to see, we discovered that the entire waterhole was void of elk with the exception of a rag-horn 4x4. At this point, we were left scrambling, trying to put together a new plan as to how and where these elk might have gone. We pulled out and headed for higher ground and started working the glasses.

We spotted some nice bulls, but not the one we were after. We spotted a big bull bedded with cows at 1,500 yards out. We hustled across, up and down these small foothill ridges to the far eastern border only to find that the bull had seen us or caught our scent and had gathered up his cows and left.

Winded, discouraged, and unsure of our next move, we started glassing and trying to catch our breath and pick up the pieces of what we thought to be our fail-proof plan. It was 8:37 A.M. when we heard a *kaboom!* followed by the whop of a well-placed shot. A sudden nausea ran through my body. I immediately turned my glasses to the direction of the shot and picked up the other hunters three ridges away. We dropped down and made our way over to see if we could help, and also to see which bull they had taken. We ran across his friend a few hundred yards before we got to the hunter. He told me they killed a nice 7x7. He said it was big and it was one of the two they had picked out as top shooters. My heart sank, but we pressed on.

We dropped down the ridge and came upon the hunter. The bull was lying in a little gully. We could only see the antler tips sticking out. We congratulated him, gave him a high five, walked over, and listened to his story. Pat stepped over the edge of the ridge, and I could see the relief in his smile. The bull the other hunter had killed was a big bruiser, but it wasn't the one we were after. A new sense of calm came over me.

We walked back to the truck; it was now 10:30 A.M. and 95°F. We ate a sandwich and began to formulate a new plan. We went back to camp, rested, played with the boys and relaxed a bit more. At 4 P.M. we headed back out. It was hot and the wind was blowing 15 mph, rendering our morning ambush spot useless. We retreated to our scouting spot under the big oak and waited. Danyelle joined us that evening as she had done so often during scouting.

As we waited, watching, and glassing, she spotted a lone bull 800 yards away under a tree. I took a quick glance with my Swarovkis, but did not put the spotting scope on him. I said, "That's a good bull, but the one we are looking for is with 30 cows. He's bigger and has ivory tips." We then glassed up quite a few bulls with small bands of cows, but saw no big bull with a big harem.

With 45 minutes of shooting time remaining, I walked to where Pat had been glassing under the next tree. We both sat there scratching our heads wondering where that monster had gone. I showed him the bull Dani had spotted on the hill. He had now gotten up and was slowly making his way to the water.

Pat said, "He's nice!" and put the spotting scope on him. Seconds later he said, "You better have a look at him."

I looked and instantly recognized those big white tips. We marked him just below the crest of the ridge and dropped everything

but our glasses and muzzleloader and flew down off the hill, as we were running out of time.

We arrived at the spot where we thought he would be past, but he was nowhere in sight. Hot, sweaty and panting again, we stood scratching our heads. We were on a small knoll between two finger ridges that came together before merging and forming a small canyon that led to the water. The air was hot and stagnant with the heavy aroma of tarweed. Our legs burned from the patches of star thistles we had portaged through, as the sun began to sink below the western hills.

In a panic, we huddled up, brainstorming where this giant bull could have given us the slip. One idea was that he had doubled back and gone behind us, or maybe he was closer and faster than we thought and had undercut us and made the water. Just then, we heard the snap of an old dry oak limb. At the sound, the hair on the back of my neck stood up. I inadvertently dropped my shooting sticks and slowly turned, and looked into the gully to my right. The tips of a big bull were coming towards us. I pulled back the hammer. He was in the very bottom and had no idea we were there. He walked within 47 yards of us. From my uphill vantage point, I could see that on his mid-section he had taken a pretty good poke in the ribs since I had last seen him the night before. That explained why he was alone and moving so slowly. He was now less than 20 yards away.

I could hear him panting in the hot evening air and could smell the rut on him. I put my sights behind his front shoulder, took a deep breath and squeezed. *Bawhoom!* barked my Remington .50-caliber, and the hill was instantly covered with a thick, white smoke. I dropped to the ground to get below it. The ground was hot and dusty.

I saw the bull swiftly running uphill and thought, *How could I have missed him?* Just then, he turned to the right, quartering toward me, and I could see a dark purplish red spot right where I had aimed, and I was thankful and relieved at the same time. As the smoke cleared, we watched him go over the ridge and heard him crash. High fives, handshakes, and hugs and a quick glance at the watch showed less than a minute before shooting time was over.

We were all in awe of this massive creature. He was beautiful and by far the largest animal I had ever taken. As twilight turned to night and the full moon rose and smiled down upon us, I felt blessed that I was able to take such an incredible bull, and that my family and friends were there to help and share in this once-in-a-lifetime adventure.

Living the Dream

Timothy R. Carpenter

California Roosevelt's Elk | Current Rank #2

HUNTING ELK IN MY HOME STATE OF CALIFORNIA HAS BEEN A dream of mine since I started hunting at the age of 12. For the last 14 years, I have applied to hunt all of the big game species in California, never missing a single year. Each year the results of the drawing left me disappointed, until this year. I found out the results were up early, and I finished my work so I could go home to check. I had drawn one of the few, and highly coveted, Roosevelt's elk tags in California.

CIRCA
2011

When I was 18, I moved to northern California to study wildlife management at Humboldt State University. I was excited to be on the north coast, so I could capitalize on my love of the outdoors. When I became a senior, I chose to study the herd dynamics of the Roosevelt's elk in the area. While I was working on my project, I realized that one area in particular had the potential for producing big Roosevelt's elk. The herd's genetics were first-class. During and after my project, I spent a total of six years photographing and videotaping these magnificent animals.

I was lucky enough to have drawn my tag in the area I had studied and gotten to know the herd so well. Most of the land in that unit was under private ownership, and the area where I spent most of my time observing and photographing was private. There are a number of landowners that would allow me to hunt for a trespass fee, but their rates were higher than I could really afford or justify. I never considered access fees when I applied for the hunt, and once I got the tag, it quickly became a stressful reality. I was unsure that I could afford to hunt the area I knew held the largest bulls.

I spent the next two months talking with numerous landowners and checking out every inch of the hunt area. My good luck continued, and I was able to secure access to a great place to hunt. It seemed as though everything was too good to be true; things were panning out just as I had always envisioned. My hunt area wasn't a large tract of land, but I knew the odds of taking a trophy bull were high. My tag allowed for any legal method of take, and since I had 12 days to hunt, I decided it was the perfect opportunity to use my bow. The thought of harvesting my first elk in an area with such great genetics using archery equipment was an exciting prospect, and my anticipation was very high.

I started scouting well before the season started. The hunt area was relatively close to my home, so I was able to spend a lot of time photographing and videotaping. I wanted to know the area like the back of my hand and have the bulls patterned as best as I could. Mornings in my hunt area were typically cold, foggy, and wet. The terrain consisted of open meadows leading up to a spruce and redwood forest with patches of alders, thick salmonberries, and blackberry thickets—perfect terrain for ambushing a big bull. Game trails and elk sign were everywhere.

While scouting, I observed two bulls that were of the caliber I was looking for. One was an absolute giant 6x7 with a 22-inch crown point and main beams that were pushing 55 inches. He was not heavy but had incredible length and character. He had been the herd bull the week before I started religiously scouting my hunt area. The second bull was a heavy 8x9 with unbelievable character and had displaced the 6x7 as the dominant bull in the herd. It was very exciting and almost surreal to contemplate that I might be presented with an opportunity to choose between the two. At times I felt greedy as I tried to talk myself through the pros and cons of each of these two bulls, either of which anyone would be rightfully proud to take and would be the bull of a lifetime.

The week before my hunt, I scouted daily, trying to keep tabs on the herd and be in a position to predict their next move first thing on opening day. I found the main herd three times that week with the 8x9 tending his cows. One foggy morning, just days prior to the opener, I found the herd, but the big bull was nowhere to be seen. Satellite bulls were herding the cows and sparring with one another. My heart sank as I pondered the fate of the big bull. *Had he been poached? Gored by another bull?* Regardless, I thought he was dead for sure.

After a few hours of desperate glassing, he rejoined the herd out of nowhere, and the smaller bulls quickly assumed their position at the periphery of the herd. The evening before opener, the herd was feeding just 300 yards from my location. I felt confident that I had patterned them well enough to predict their location on opening morning.

I contacted my brother Don and told him to make the trek north. He arrived at 2 A.M. after a six-hour drive to hunt with me on opening day. Needless to say, neither of us got much sleep that night.

Opening morning arrived, and it was foggy and wet. Just after first light, I saw the herd moving from where I had last seen them. My friend John and my brother Don were with me. Don was running the video camera, as we were hoping to get everything on film. Things were happening much faster than I had anticipated, but I quickly got into position. The entire herd, more than 50, was within 40 to 100 yards of where I set up, but the herd bull was obscured in the middle. Two 300-class 6x6 satellite bulls came within 20 yards trying to get near the cows. It was very exciting to have that much action on the first morning of my hunt! I never had a clear shot at the herd bull before they fed out of range and eventually bedded down. Unfortunately, Don had to head back to work after just the first day, so I lost my main hunting partner.

On the third day of my hunt, my friends Kevin and Chris joined me. We did a small hike, glassing meticulously and calling occasionally. By 10 A.M., we hadn't seen any elk or heard a single bugle. We sat down and cow-called for a little while. Out of the brush came a large black bear. He was moving along a trail and eating blackberries. I had a bear tag, and the season was open, so I decided to make a move. He was a big bear and looked to be between 300 and 350 pounds. With the camera rolling, I started the stalk and got within 25 yards. He was just on the other side of an alder thicket and decided to take a different path than I had anticipated. As quickly as he came in, he was gone. We got the entire stalk on film, and in hindsight, watching the bear take the upper fork in the trail was almost comical. It was an exciting twist to a relatively uneventful morning.

That evening, my girlfriend Heidi came with me. We located the herd and closely watched every move the herd bull made. As we sat behind a log, glassing, yellow jackets started swarming around us. It turned out that we were sitting on a ground hive! Luckily, neither of us got stung. Unfortunately, the herd spent the remainder of the day safely out of reach.

On the fourth day, I hunted alone. At sunrise, the lead cow showed the herd the way. I quickly took position behind an old redwood log. As the cows started funneling past me at 20 yards, I knew the herd bull wouldn't be too far behind. He was in full rut, letting off bone-trembling bugles and chasing off other bulls. I knew that my chance was almost here, and I would have a shot between 5 and 20 yards. I peered over the log and saw him running at me in a full sprint. In a flash, he covered over 200 yards.

He stopped just 20 yards from me, and as he grunted, steam bellowed from his nostrils and mouth. Wide-eyed, he looked to the left and right, and then put his head down and started thrashing the ground with his huge antlers; dirt and grass were flying everywhere. I slowly lowered myself, nocked an arrow, and hunkered down, waiting for him to cross between the log I was hiding behind and

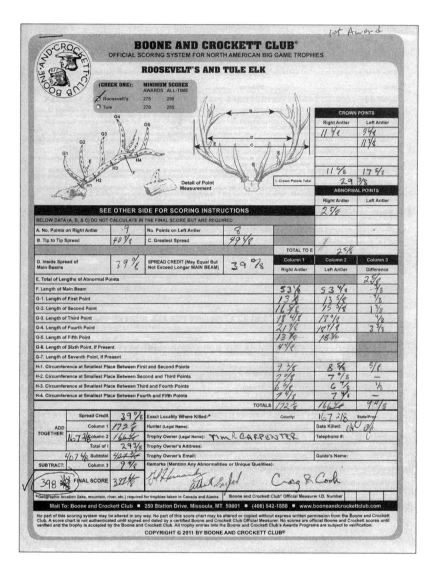

a patch of impenetrable blackberry brambles just 20 yards away. I waited for a solid minute then peered through a crack in the end of the log. He had run back the 200 yards and was standing with the other half of the herd. In the process of the sneak peak I took, I spooked all of the cows and calves and blew my cover. I thought I had totally ruined what could have been my only shot.

I watched the drama unfold in the herd. As satellite bulls in the 300-class tried to get near the cows, the herd bull chased them off. The herd was on the move, and they seemed to be on edge—there was a lot of tension. The rut was in full swing for the first day since the hunt started. The herd cow was uneasy and wanted to make her way back towards me.

To my amazement, the herd started to cross back, this time, a couple hundred yards from where I had set up. I knew that I had to move quickly or they would disappear into the thick salmonberries. Most of the herd were making their way back around the base of the hill when the herd bull stopped pushing the cows around, put his head down, and started to feed out of sight. I knew he wouldn't be feeding for long, so I decided to make a quick and risky move.

I had no way to get within range without moving through an opening in plain view of some of the cows. It was my only shot, so I took it. As I moved through, I startled a dozen or so cows and calves, hoping to get to the bull before he realized that I was there. I quickly closed the distance and got into a position just 12 yards from the quartering bull. I didn't have time to range him, but I knew he was close. I drew back, settled in my pin and released. I made a solid hit, and the shaft of my arrow was buried up to the fletchings. The bull didn't know what hit him. He trotted off, herding his cows for the next few seconds. He was down within 30 yards from where I had shot him. I couldn't have asked for a better hunt, and I think I am still in shock as to how it all turned out.

When I finally placed my hands on the bull for the first time, it truly set in. I'm still in awe and can't believe that I was able to take the pending new World's Record Roosevelt's elk with a bow. He officially measured at 398-1/8 B&C. I want to thank all of my friends and family that put up with my passion for hunting and for all their support over the years.

Sharing the Experience

Taking to the field with friends and family creates a strong sense of community and furthers our continent's strong sense of our hunting heritage. It's also a way to pass down skills and generate enthusiasm for wildlife and the outdoors. Lifelong bonds are forged over campfires and through teamwork and determination in the field. Most hunters will tell you this is the most important part of their hunting experiences; the animal harvested is only secondary.

Mexico's Wild Desert Sheep

Alberto Tapia Landeros

Mexico Desert Sheep | Current Rank #20

SINCE BOYHOOD I HAD HEARD AND READ STORIES ABOUT SHEEP hunting. My favorite storyteller was, and is, Mr. Jack O'Connor.

In my early life as a hunter, I knew I would never have the chance to hunt any sheep species other than the desert rams of my home state. So I made a promise to look for the best head in the mountains near my home, in Mexicali, Baja California, Mexico—and with a little luck, maybe a chance in the Sonoran Mountains, the same hunting place where O'Connor took his best desert sheep.

CIRCA **1973**

First, my goal was to take a better head than that of the celebrated outdoor writer. In the process, I became eager to write hunting adventures too, in the style of O'Connor and Hemingway. This story represents my third attempt to publish in English. The other two appeared in *Petersen's Hunting Magazine Deer Annual* in the early '80s.

The early '70s was the era of the Winchester pre-1964 bolt-action rifles in .270 Winchester caliber. That was my father's rifle, from whom I inherited the passion for sheep hunting. That was O'Connor's caliber for hunting mountain sheep—and mine too. The ultra velocity guns that started to appear in the field didn't attract our

From left to right, the author's father Alberto Tapia Yanez, Policarpio Alvarez Romero and the author, cooking the liver of his best mule deer taken in Baja California. Photographed by the author's brother Armando Tapia Landeros.

attention those days, almost half a century ago. Back then we didn't know about magnum cartridges or sheep census and populations.

In those days, we never saw a sheep hunting permit. Once in a while we heard of a foreign hunter, Mexican or non-Mexican, who came to our mountains and shot one or several animals, ewes included. In some cases, they had a letter from some federal official to permit the "hunting." O'Connor said that the one he used to hunt in Sonora was signed by a high-range military official. Besides, in those years, sheep hunting had been banned since 1922. These practices have nothing to do with modern management. Those hunters were important or very rich people, not local hunters like me, and I was not alone. Several riflemen from Baja and Sonora had the same passion for mountain sheep hunting, and we all did the same thing: study the sheep's habitat, organize the hunt, climb the mountains, glass the country, hunt alone without a guide, shoot, skin the trophy, take the game out of the mountains on our backs, and in my case, even mount the trophy and write the story.

I have always had great respect for those solitary early local meat hunters. They didn't use spotting and rifle scopes, camo dressing, GPS, maps, radio or cell phones, and they never knew any permit or heard about the animal's population estimations. They hunted for a living; to bring home the bacon. In the process, they took some outstanding heads. That was the case of the All-time World's Record for desert sheep, the 205-1/8 B&C points credited to Carl Scrivens but taken by a local "vaquero" in 1940, when sheep hunting was still banned. In 1964 the ban on sheep hunting in Mexico ended, but sheep tags were never required for local Baja and Sonora hunters.

Every hunter dreams about a record head. In 1971, my father took a very good ram, a 186 green measurement in the field—bigger than that of O'Connor's—and I decided not to shoot a lesser pair of horns. Recently, my father's ram was measured by a Boone and Crockett Official Measurer at 182-4/8 points. With a bit of luck, both heads will appear on the same first page of the desert sheep category of the All-time records book in 2017.

One autumn afternoon in 1972, a professional meat hunter and my father's friend, Pablo Martinez, told us that in Arroyo Grande, Sierra de Juarez, Baja California, a very big ram was spotted by Policarpio Álvarez Romero, a cowboy for the American cattleman Enrique Jolliff. We knew that country very well, and we knew it could produce trophy-sized mule deer too, so we decided to hunt in that direction. On the 5th of January 1973, we intended to camp in the high desert area of Arroyo Grande, but an early snow obliged us to descend and camp in lower hill country. That natural event put me on a collision course with my ram and is responsible for me being here telling my hunting story.

The author's late friend and top sheep guide Jesus Aguiar Martinez with the record ram hunted by J.C. McElroy in 1978 in Arroyo Grande, Baja California. Although its horns measure 29-1/8 inches from tip-to-tip ranking in the top 10 for spread, the final score is only 176-3/8 B&C points.

The next day, my brother Armando and my father took the course of the "in-between" creek. In a north Baja map or in Google maps, you can locate this place between the famous Arroyo Grande Canyon, and the Jaquejel Canyon. Because of that geographical position we named this place the "In-between Canyon." A friend from San Felipe, Baja California, Dr. Ubaldo Espinoza, and I took the hill route to Arroyo Grande. Soon we found oxidized sardine, tuna and fruit juice cans, typical food of Mexican "borregueros" (sheepherders). I told my friend, "Here is more likely we see sheep than deer." And my memory took me to the big ram that Policarpio had seen in this area.

We heard sheep coughing. Later, sheep of all ages filed out of the arroyo in front of us. We glassed them and found no trophies. I told Ubaldo to cautiously walk to the rim of the hill to see if some rams were still there. The doctor approached the spot, holding one of my lightweight mountain rifles, a Husqvarna Sporter in 7x57 caliber, topped with a Leupold compact 4x scope. Then we heard the characteristic hoofs and stone sounds of sheep on the run and waited. One huge ram came out very close, about 80 meters. I shouldered my rifle and saw through the Redfield Wide Field 4x scope the biggest ram I had ever seen.

I decided to shoot that great animal, with a hint of hope that it was Policarpio's big ram. After the sound of the Silvertip 130-grain bullet exiting the 24-inch barrel, the mountain monarch fell in its tracks. I put my rifle aside and thanked God for the opportunity of encountering such an animal. I inspected it—an old ram, with full and massive horns, very thin neck and worn teeth. The left ear had a scar, maybe a bite of a predator when young. A notorious scar without hair in the top of its shoulder that when skinned showed the main apophasis bone broken by a bullet. Some unlucky hunter overshot and lost "my ram" years earlier. Maybe at close range, too.

Our first field measurement green-scored above 190 B&C points. Forty years later, my ram scored 188-1/8 B&C points. Time takes its toll. The Matson Laboratories of California analyzed a tooth of this animal and concluded that it died at 8 years of age. But its looks misled even a seasoned biologist who opined that it was 16 years old. Rams do not live long lives.

In 1974, the Mexican Federal Program of Bighorn Sheep started, and I ended my sheep hunting career. In the first hunting expedition, and at some hundred meters from the place I shot my ram, American hunter John B. Solo and guide Aureliano Caro found in a cave the skeleton of a huge ram that biologist Ticul Alvarez measured at 202 B&C points. This head has never been officially measured, but it could be Policarpio's ram. Arroyo Grande produces big ones. In 1978, J.C. McElroy, founder of Safari Club International, took the spread record ram: 29-1/8 tip-to-tip spread.

In 1981, my good friend and guide Jesus Aguiar, guided Bruno Sherrer, an American hunter who took a ram scoring 191-1/8 B&C points in this same place. Some few kilometers south, Javier Lopez Del Bosque bagged a ram that a Mexican official measured at 196 B&C points, but eight years later officially appeared in the records book with 192-7/8. Time took its toll again. During helicopter monitoring in 2010 by the University of Baja California and Dr. Raymond Lee, a huge ram was observed in the Arroyo Grande area again. Witnesses assure that its horns are 200 B&C points-plus. In this same place I shot my best striped-tail mule deer in 1972. Currently, I'm proposing that this area is declared a sanctuary for deer and sheep.

Between 1976 and 1978, I directed a federal program to build water reservoirs for desert sheep in the north part of the state of Baja California. Following the California and Arizona trend, our work provided several water catch impoundments in the most arid parts of sheep habitat, the San Felipe Desert.

I worked as an environmental advisor for the former Governor of Baja California, Eugenio Elorduy, whose administration created Mexico's equivalent to the U.S. Environmental Protection Agency. Now, the federal government will be able to manage the wild game for people of Baja California. In the following years, the hunting permits, sheep tags included, will be issued and managed by Baja Californians. An idea that I started to develop in 1973, when I worked in the state government, is now a reality 40 years later. A long war fought and won. During the 22 years of no legal hunting in Baja, the sheep population increased by 56 percent—another positive effect of opposing the over-hunting situation that prevailed in the late 80s.

The good news was announced in November 2011 at the "University and Sheep Congress" that I organized with some of the past deans of the University of Baja California.

On February 23, 1996, the Foundation for North American Wild Sheep (now the Wild Sheep Foundation) recognized my efforts toward sheep conservancy with the organization's Presidential Award in Reno, Nevada. The plaque reads: "For your effort and dedication to bring professional management and long-term survivability to Mexico's wild desert sheep." Now, the Boone and Crockett Club has recognized my best sheep taken in a brief period as a sheep hunter (1965 to 1973). I'm very grateful to the Boone and Crockett Club for maintaining the records of our big game animals, archives that are invaluable for researchers and environmental historians.

I hope that these 22 years of no legal sheep hunting in Baja bring new and outstanding opportunities to take trophy desert sheep in my home state. I hope, too, that the chances run equal for residents and nonresident hunters. Only with the participation and support of the local hunters, the future of hunting our great sheep can be sustainable.

Our Grizzly Hunt

Roger J. Pentecost

British Columbia Grizzly Bear | Current Rank #4

J ASON, MY SON, WAS THEN 12 YEARS OLD; THIS WAS TO BE OUR first "real" hunt. He had hunted since he was seven years old, around our ranch in southern B.C. We had decided on grizzly. I had always wanted a trophy grizzly. I had ranched some years before in the Anahim Lake area. We had friends there, and we knew there were large bears in the area.

CIRCA
1982

With weeks set-aside, we packed our guns. Jason chose a single-shot Savage Model 219L in .30-30 caliber, with a 4x Weaver scope. I chose my .270 caliber Husqvarna with a 2.5-8x Bausch & Lomb scope.

After arriving in the Anahim Lake area, we went a few days visiting and talking about bears, and hunting moose. We contacted Wayne Escott, who had worked for me in the early '70s and was now a commercial bush pilot for Dean River Air. We made a deal to get the floatplane from Monday, October 11 until October 16. We had heard the stories of big bear down on the Bella Coola River, but some of the Indians talked of "Good Bear" along the nearly inaccessible Dean River mouth where it meets the Dean Channel.

On Monday morning, we left Nimpo Lake and flew down southwest over Charlotte Lake, then heading west to Lonesome Lake, circling to take photos of the very impressive Hunlen Falls that drop straight down about 1,000 feet and flow into the Atnarko River. I had wanted to see these falls for a long time. We then headed north, stopping for lunch and so Jason could fish at Squiness Lake, named after an old-time Indian family of the area.

We arrived late that afternoon in the Dean Channel. Pulling up on a sandbar at the river mouth, we unloaded the plane and made camp right there. We had already found tracks, so our excitement was starting to build. The next day we moved the plane along the river bank about 300 yards and on the south side, so as to be beside our camp. Starting out, we got across the river and worked our way up the shoreline. Wayne knew Felix, an 80-year old Swedish recluse, who had been living in near isolation for many years there.

We took Felix a moose meat roast as a gift, and got into a long conversation with him about life, bears, etc. He told of mushroom hunters landing there by plane, and picking up to $1,000 per trip, each, with the mushrooms being sold in Japan. We scouted that area quite a bit, finding sign of bear but not seeing any of the real thing.

On Wednesday, Jason and I left early, ready for bear. We went south, down the channel, finding sign but nothing else. The banks along this channel were steep and made the going really tough. We saw seal out in the water, and a lot of eagles, but still no bears. We worked our way back inland, arriving about a half-mile upriver from camp, where we found really promising sign and country, but that was all.

Thursday was cold and damp, but not freezing, yet. We had made up our minds that we would go up river on the south side. Wayne, our pilot, was going to come along, having fiddled enough with the plane the day before. The going was really slow and tough. It seemed that for every 10 feet forward, we would also go 10 feet sideways, first down into the river edge, which was usually covered with masses of tangled logs, then up along the very steep banks above the river. There we were, climbing over dead trees and inching our way along. The thought never really occurred to me as to how I would get back with a bear, if we got "lucky".

About mid-morning, we stopped to snack. Jason had found a simply enormous bear track in a sandy bay area tucked into the river edge, and we speculated over lunch at the size of the bear that made that track. It was surely a "good bear." We could not see up or down the river more than 100 yards.

About then, we heard a Super Cub drifting low and slow, as they are so good at. For a brief moment, it flashed in front of us, coming down stream and passing out toward where our plane sat. I cursed under my breath, thinking that I hadn't come all this way to have any bear spooked right out of the area by people when we were 100 miles from a village and even farther from a town.

With a little more uncertainty, but still the same enthusiasm, we started off, crossing a small side channel and re-wetting ourselves for at least the 10th time (or so it seemed). After a while, I decided to move away from the river's main course. Soon we were walking in a succession of semi-clearings, under some enormous cedar trees that shut out most of the direct sunlight. The flickering shadows across the leafy carpet gave a shady, peaceful look to the area.

Suddenly, off to our left about 70 feet away and partly obscured by a cedar, something started to move slowly up out of the ground. It was a massive head in profile, followed by an enormous shoulder bump. We froze. Here was what we had come all this way for, "a good bear." But really, I never wanted it quite so close. As I readied my Husqvarna, I heard Jason close his gun.

For what seemed to be a long time, I had an excellent side shot. I squeezed the shot off. But, the bear, instead of falling over dead, rose up out of the hollow in the ground and turned toward us. Here it was, coming right at us. I aimed at his shoulder, still hardly believing he wasn't down. This next shot hit his side, I had gut shot him. This turned him, and he plunged off sideways into a really thick area of alders, windfalls, and devils club. As he was going in, I placed a third shot.

All hell seemed to break loose in that small wooded area. It was too thick to see what was happening, but boy, could we hear the bear snorting, growling, grunting, and gasping draughts of breath. It was a simply enormous and rather frightening sound. I looked back at Jason and Wayne. They looked as apprehensive as I felt. I knew a grizzly could explode out of that cover like an "express train", with none of the bush slowing him down at all, and leap 15 feet in a bound.

I indicated to the others that I was going to circle around, hoping I could get to a point for a fatal shot. Using some of the larger trees as cover, I circled from tree to tree in the best John Wayne style, but without his air of confidence. Jason and Wayne were following me. All of us were feeling very naked, only knowing where the bear was by that horrific noise. At last, I could see part of the bear's rear.

At this point, I swapped guns with Jason for the final shot as I had used three of my five bullets. He had all six that he carried left. I was finally about 20 ft. away from the bear, feeling—to be honest—quite scared. I placed the fatal shot into his neck with Jason's .30-30. As it lay dead, I could see that we had a very "good bear" indeed. But why had my first shot not killed it?

When I skinned it out later, I could see the bullet hole in the exact spot I had aimed, but the Nosler bullet had shattered before getting deep enough in such a large bear. I also found a tight, leather radio collar around his neck. It was well into his fur, and had rubbed sore marks on either side of his neck. I felt bad now, knowing that the bear I had shot was part of a study. But, what was it doing here, 50 miles from any closed area? Thinking back on this, I did not see the collar, even when close to the bear. Plus, with us walking up on him, I don't know if the bear would have given us the choice of letting him, or us, walk away.

We started the task of skinning, still in awe of this great trophy bear. The skinning went slowly, and we were only about half-finished when Wayne pointed out that it was about an hour before sunset. So, with great apprehension, we left the partially finished bear. With some knowledge of the best route back, we made it to camp just at darkness. We had nervously picked our way, expecting to meet another bear at every turn.

That night, I had many mixed thoughts. Some were good and some terrible. I'd really shot a "good bear," but there was the matter of the number of shots, the collar, and worst of all, leaving him there. *What if coyote, fox, wolf, wolverine, eagle got to him?* All these "what ifs" kept coming back to me. We consoled ourselves that at least another grizzly would not eat it.

That night, we had entertainment of a nature that we didn't need. It started with some splashing and grunts that sounded all too close. *Were they just trying to find salmon carcasses, or were they looking for us?* We built the fire up high, and in the light of it, pulled in some more of the washed-up logs scattered around real close. Supper was welcome, but the food seemed to dry out and stick as it went down my throat. Even Jason noticed the tension. Normally, good food and sleep would be the only thing on his mind by now, but that night he was making sure that he could sleep in the middle of the tent.

It seemed that all through the night, the bears were getting closer. Wayne and I agreed that we would take turns to keep the fire going. Morning drifted in, as a cold, damp blanket of mist, leaving everything dripping. Jason walked over toward the river, about 20 feet from the tent area where we were preparing breakfast and coffee. His face told us that he had seen something. "Look! Quick, over there in the river are three more bears, not 200 yards from our camp," he said. They were poking around in the river, looking for their breakfast. We could have shot any one of them, with one looking as big as ours, right in camp!

We didn't discuss it, but I was feeling worried as to what would await us back at the bear site. Soon, we had the packboard, rope and some lunch ready and we were off. Wayne felt he should carry his .30-30 Winchester, "just in case." We set out up the river, with the three bears noted earlier nowhere to be seen. We tried to make quite a bit of noise and took our path out in the open as much as possible. Things had done a 180-degree turn from yesterday. I really hoped that our furry friends would stay away today.

A couple of ravens flew up as we approached the bear, but no

eagles were in evidence. A quick examination showed the hide to be perfect, so we got down to work. Only now was the size of this bear really impacting on me. Just lifting his paws, and looking around at the havoc he had wrought, made me even more respectful of his massive power.

I had skinned out many moose while I was guiding, and also cows on the ranch, but trying to turn over and move 1,000 pounds of grizzly is tough. We pushed, pulled, shoved and did just about everything we could think of to turn him over. Boy, what a job. I had cut the skull off at the neck joint, and the paws at the wrist bones, thinking that I would do the rest in Anahim Lake the next day. We rolled up the skin, with the feet, paws and head inside, and proceeded to rope it onto the packboard. Then I tried to lift it and get it on my back. That didn't work. Wayne and I carried the packboard over to a large cedar, lifted it up to shoulder height, and with Wayne's help, I swung it on. Hell, it just about swung me down with it. I tightened the waist belt, and with Jason carrying my .270, we started back.

Things went well, until we came to the first downed tree. As I tried to get over, the pack and bear skin pulled me backward. It was no use, I couldn't hike out with this massive weight. I decided the only way was to skin the head and paws out, and generally flesh-out the hide. Two hours later, we were ready to continue. We had lost at least 50 pounds from the load, and when re-packed, I felt that I could just manage it. Boy, what a journey back to camp. I was glad we were only three miles in.

After a quick lunch, we broke camp and loaded the plane. This is when our next excitement began. The tide in the inlet was down; consequently, the river level at the mouth had fallen. It was too shallow for take-off with all the weight, so we unloaded the plane. I waded out into the river, holding the plane straight up stream as I stumbled around in the ice water. With the plane as light as possible and the motor warm, Wayne gave it full throttle. My heart was in my mouth as Wayne, in his expert manner, bounced the plane up the river, until first one and then the other float lifted and he disappeared round the bend. Moments later, we were pleased to see the plane lift up above the trees, as it wheeled round grabbing for height to get over the trees. It was then I realized my legs were damned cold, I was still standing out in the cold, rushing water.

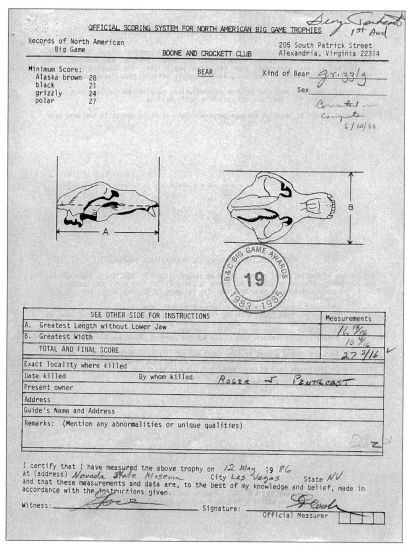

George Lackerd
1st Awd

OFFICIAL SCORING SYSTEM FOR NORTH AMERICAN BIG GAME TROPHIES

Records of North American
Big Game

BOONE AND CROCKETT CLUB

205 South Patrick Street
Alexandria, Virginia 22314

Minimum Score:
Alaska brown 28
black 21
grizzly 24
polar 27

BEAR

Kind of Bear *grizzly*

Sex

Corrected in Computer 6/10/86

B&C BIG GAME AWARDS 19 1983-1985

SEE OTHER SIDE FOR INSTRUCTIONS	Measurements
A. Greatest Length without Lower Jaw	16 14/16
B. Greatest Width	10 4/16
TOTAL AND FINAL SCORE	27 2/16 ✓

Exact locality where killed

Date killed | By whom killed *Roger J. Pentecost*

Present owner

Address

Guide's Name and Address

Remarks: (Mention any abnormalities or unique qualities)

I certify that I have measured the above trophy on *12 May* 19 *86*
at (address) *Nevada State Museum* City *Las Vegas* State *NV*
and that these measurements and data are, to the best of my knowledge and belief, made in
accordance with the instructions given.

Witness: _____ Signature: _____
Official Measurer

Wayne landed out in the channel, then taxied in to the sandbar that we had started this hunt from. Packing our equipment on the plane went well, as I thought of warm baths and scotch whiskey that was waiting at Anahim Lake. A half-hour later, we were skimming over the lake infested timber. We landed at Nimpo Lake. We were soon at Darcy Christensen's village store, where we related the story for the first of many times.

Darcy, our host, had a country butcher's shop out back, and a 500-pound scale with a meat hook hung high. Two of us hoisted up my grizzly and watched as the needle pointed to 148 pounds. Next, we weighed the undressed skull; it was 45 pounds, so we assumed that with the paws, etc., the hide had weighed over 200 pounds. No wonder it was so impossible to pack any distance over that rough going.

We got to work, spreading out the bear and then working coarse salt into the hide. We spent lots of time on the ears, releasing the cartilage right up to the tips and getting the salt in. From the measurements that we took, we worked out that the bear stood over 10-feet, 6-inches high and could have reached over 13 feet. The rug has a 9-foot, 6-inch spread, with claws longer than my fingers.

This was far more of a grizzly than I had ever dreamed of getting. As we retired that night, we went over bear stories such as the Anahim Lake rancher and neighbor, Cony King, who had been attacked by a grizzly sow and now sports a blank eye socket and massive scars from this near fatal encounter.

It was April 1983 when I got an excited phone call from Helmut Schold, a young German émigré taxidermist who had impressed me with his skill and artistic ability. He had been so shocked by the finished size of the skull that he had taken it to Helmut Cofmeister, a Government Wildlife Technician. They had green-scored the skull length at 17 inches with a skull width of 10-5/16 inches, giving a total score of 27-5/16, which put it over the existing world's record. On June 21, 1983, Jack Graham and Jim Laughton, both Boone and Crockett Official Measurers, met with grizzly and me for an official measuring. Ultimately, my bear received an official B&C score of 27-2/16 inches by B&C's 19th Big Game Awards Judges Panel.

Jason and I have reflected on this hunt on several occasions, still only half believing that his first major hunt could end this way. For us, it simply remains "our grizzly hunt."

The Fold

Donald F. Blake

Minnesota Canada Moose | Current Rank #8

M Y MOOSE HUNT STARTED DURING THE SUMMER OF 1985 WHEN I found out that I had been drawn for a coveted Minnesota state moose license. Roughly four percent of the applicants are successful in the alternate, odd-year hunts. Minnesota assigns four hunters to the single license for one moose. On my license were my wife, Darlene, and two close friends.

CIRCA **1985**

Preparations for the hunt started at this time. Darlene and I decided that if we were fortunate enough to take a moose, to have a plaque mount made rather than full head mount. We felt that most moose mounts are rather ugly and very imposing on a room. Two scouting trips were made by Darlene and me. Even being in this area of the Superior National Forest (less than five miles from the Boundary Waters Canoe Area) is exciting; one never knows what will be found around the next corner, deer, black bear, or a moose. For the five years previous to my moose hunt, I had been hunting grouse and black bear, and encountering moose in this area. Encounters with bull moose at this time of year are not always the most pleasant, such as being forced to drive backward down a one-lane logging trail with a moose chasing you.

We started the hunt with very high hopes but we were down

to three hunters (one friend could not make it) and after the first weekend, we were down to two hunters, Darlene and me. Our hopes remained high but after nine solid days of hunting, both Darlene and I had to return to our jobs. By mid-week, I planned to return alone.

I was feeling highly frustrated, as we had not yet filled our tag. We had passed up a cow, had been within 30 yards of a moose in a spruce bog and were not able to see it, and we blew a stalk on two bulls with 50-inch plus racks that were fighting in a swampy area during a snow squall. I had tried many different types of hunting: still, stand, drives, grunting, and rattling of antlers (I had found an antler in a spruce bog) without success. At this point, I was feeling so frustrated that if I had thought that it would help, I would have sat down and cried.

On Wednesday, I returned to the Baker Lake campsite by myself, too late to hunt. Thursday, the weather was the best of the whole hunt, bright sunshine, gusty winds, and temperature in the 60s. After hunting all morning, I drove 20 miles to the Minnesota Department of Natural Resources Moose Registration Station in Tofte Minnesota to check the status of the hunt. Fourteen of the 16 tags in the zone had been filled. I also called my wife to let her know that I had arrived okay. She told me that our dog, Floyd, had died the night before. This did not help my enthusiasm.

I made a decision to check an old clear-cut area, 20 miles up the Caribou Trail. We had not hunted this area, but we had scouted there and had seen a lot of sign. It looked like a wintering area for moose. Time was running out, just over three days of hunting were left. All these things were weighing on me as I started to still hunt the edge of the clear-cut.

Suddenly, to my left, something caught my eye, white on black and about 200 yards out. Grabbing my binoculars, I muttered "Oh my God, he's huge."

Here was the largest bull I had ever seen. Before I could react, the bull disappeared. Running up a hill, I came out about 75 yards above him. Shaking, I took a shot and heard my .30-06 hand-loaded bullet impact. The bull started to run and, in two steps, disappeared into the brush. Later, I found that the bullet had entered the left side, breaking a rib on the way in, had gone through the heart, both lungs, and had shattered the upper leg bone on the opposite leg, before stopping under the skin. It was a wonder that he could travel the 200 yards that he did, after being hit so solidly.

Running after him, I was so excited I didn't even know that I had run through a creek until later when I found I had wet pants and shoes. Seeing him standing, I shot again. This time he ran off, favoring his right front leg. Approaching the area where I saw him last, I could hear the rasping breath of a dying animal. I decided to wait a while longer. After it got quiet, I circled around and approached from the back side and put another round into the spine when I saw hair rising and falling (the bullet didn't even go through the spine).

Sitting down, I was admiring this beautiful animal when I imagined that I could hear God saying, "You prayed for a big moose, now here is a big moose," and then peals of laughter. Right then I knew that I had a big job ahead of me. I was able to get my four wheel drive pickup about 800 feet from the moose. Of course, I had to cross a bog, a creek, and numerous downfalls to get to my moose. I started field dressing him about 3:30 P.M. and quit about midnight. Exhausted, I collapsed into bed in the back of the pickup.

Waking at sunrise, and seeing a heavy frost on the ground, I decided to stay in bed a little longer. Around 8 o'clock, I was startled awake by timber wolves howling about 100 yards away. I was rather hoping that they would help themselves, saving me a lot of work that I knew lay ahead. I began boning-out the meat into portions small enough to pack out on my pack frame. It took the entire day to bone and pack out the meat and the hide, along with some teeth and the antlers. During the last trip out with the hide, I heard a ripping noise that I hoped wasn't my back, then, all-of-a-sudden, my pack frame broke. I could not remember being so tired from a hunt before.

At the DNR Moose Registration Station, the game biologists were excited by the size of the antlers and said that it was the largest antler set they had ever seen. The antlers were green scored at 229 B&C points. The antlers have 36 scorable points, and they are greater than 59 inches wide and 47 inches long, with the distinctive brow palms of a mature bull and a fold in the left antler. My moose was the 16th and last moose registered in that zone. During the five-hour drive home I alternated between euphoria and exhaustion.

The Minnesota DNR aged my moose at 7-1/2 years old from an examination of the teeth.

After finding out how high in the records books my moose scored, Darlene and I decided to have a full head mount done by Mid-America Taxidermy in Savage, Minnesota. Brad Reddick, the taxidermist, found a cape from an Alaska-Yukon moose and used that for our mount. There is a joke about the hunt not being the most costly part, it's the addition needed on the house to hold the trophy. Well, we could not get the mounted moose through the doors into our old house until we put in a patio door. We had the hide tanned with the hair on for a rug that we use as a comforter on our bed.

Coincidentally, during the 1987 Minnesota moose season a moose was taken within 20 miles of where I took mine that has the same distinctive fold in the left antler. That moose scores 209. Also in the fall of 1986, while grouse hunting, I met two couples that had, ironically, taken their bull moose in the early 1980s in the same exact place where I had taken my moose.

While I did not set out to take a trophy animal, I have been blessed with a hunt, memories, and an animal-of-a-lifetime. My moose has won the NRA's highest hunting award, the prestigious 1986 Leatherstocking Award, the Minnesota Deer Classic award for the largest moose taken in Minnesota, my story of the hunt was published in *Outdoor Life's 1988 Annual*, and my antlers were part of the Boone and Crockett Club's 20th Big Game Awards.

Christmas, a Day Early

William B. Bullock

Arizona Coues' Whitetail | Current Rank #28

'M NO DIFFERENT FROM ANY OTHER TROPHY HUNTER. I HUNT to see game and enjoy it, not to just fill a tag and go home. I enjoy the country and the aspects of hunting: glassing, stalking to get a closer look, studying the prey, enjoying the incidental wildlife, and simply experiencing natural treats that most non-hunters never even know exist. I'm usually successful at eventually filling my tag, but I most always know that I could have filled it sooner, had I wanted to do only that. However, I must honestly admit that I'm usually just a touch disappointed when I approach my freshly downed quarry; maybe I should have taken the one yesterday, or held out a little longer. Sure he's a nice one, but maybe, just maybe, there's a B&C trophy was out there somewhere.

CIRCA **1986**

In the late 1970s, my dad and I began to hunt Coues' whitetails, before they became popular. It seemed that every time we went hunting javelina, quail, mountain lion, or whatever, we found whitetails. Not lots of whitetails, just enough to make us think about a new hunting spot come fall.

Dad had taken a dandy buck in 1973. At 107-1/8, it made the Arizona Records Book, just missing the B&C minimum of 110. Every time I looked at that buck, I began to dream. There had to be bigger ones out there, and most people didn't really care about them.

We found a spot just north of Roosevelt Lake that had a fairly good Coues' deer population. While Arizona hunters must wade through a drawing process to hunt deer in the fall, this particular area was a cinch to get a permit for whitetails only. We had to pack in about three miles, carrying our own water and food. After the first year or two, we had our packing down to a science. While we saw bucks every year, and only one or two other hunters, we actually took only four deer in six years. None scored above the 90s. In the meantime, new hunts were being opened up during the late December rut in north-central Arizona, closer to home. A few bigger bucks were being taken, some approaching, and a few even making, the "book."

In 1985, we both drew permits and decided to give it a try. Dad took a buck midway through the season that was respectable, although still in the 90-point range. I passed up about a dozen decent bucks, looking for that rare exception. I finally took a smaller one to fill my tag on the season's final day. The sound of my rifle had just completed its final echo when I heard rocks roll and then watched a real nice Coues' buck trot off. Of course, he had to stop and look back at 80 yards. I think he even smiled. His beautiful rack would have crowded the "book." If a lion didn't get him, he would probably be there next year. But, would I?

Permits were getting tough to come by. Coues' whitetails had become popular, and not just to trophy hunters. Someone decided that those cute little deer were good eating. I eat wild game year round, and the fact is that they're really not all that good. They're usually tough and dry, and they're strong from being in the rut. But, Lady Luck again gave me a permit in 1986. Maybe this year would be different.

By opening day my hunting partner and I were excited. We still remembered the buck that trotted off on the last day of the year before. We turned on the last two-track road that would lead to "our" favorite country. As we topped the last ridge, we counted three sets of taillights a half-mile or so ahead. Two more vehicles were leaving camps not far ahead of us and heading in the same direction. Since I didn't feel properly invited to that party, I spun the Bronco around and we headed for some "new" country that we had casually looked at while scouting.

An hour later we were looking at a series of rolling pinyon pine and juniper ridges that we had never been on before. Glassing looked to be much more difficult than where we had hunted the year before, and we now had a very late start. But something about new country and opening day really gets the juices flowing. It felt good to be hunting whitetails again. It turned into quite a day. As well as seeing several bull elk, we saw over 20 Coues' deer, far more than I normally see in my style of hunting. We saw no respectable bucks, but we did see several smaller ones. We got a feel for the country that turned out to be valuable.

The next day, we had a plan of attack. We climbed to a fairly high vantage point that gave us about a 200° view, including the heads of two juniper-covered basins. Glassing was tedious. My partner, Steve, and I would spot a deer. That same deer would vanish in the thick trees in seconds, leaving us with strained vision while trying to detect even parts of other deer in that area. I studied likely looking places for as much as 30 minutes, only to see a deer that had been there all along step into view and then disappear again in seconds, leaving me to wonder if I had really seen him at all. Meanwhile, Steve had spotted three does in the open, feeding near a rocky outcropping some distance away.

While Steve is a good hunter, he chose to stay with hunting mule deer for meat. Blessed with an exceptional set of eyes, and being a good friend, I have found him to be very helpful in looking for that special buck and in keeping the hunt lively. I'm sure that many times he has asked himself what in the world I'm waiting for. Moments later, he knew.

It was Steve who spotted the buck. I quickly set up the spotting scope. The eyepiece showed a mass of antlers. I didn't know how many points. I simply stated, "That's him." My next move is normally a stalk.

Steve and I discussed it. We could get to the rocky outcropping, but we would take a chance of spooking the three does and probably never see the buck. The other direction was out of the question, too low. Due to the lay of the land, a move in any direction to shorten the distance would cut off our view. We had to try it from there. We guessed the distance at 450 yards.

I knew that the Remington 7mm Mag. could do the job, I just didn't know if I could. I have to admit I was nervous. I found a rest, and Steve set up to call the location of my shots, should I miss. I settled the crosshairs until they lay right on the buck's back. My instincts told me to hold higher, but I have always believed that I should never hold off an animal on the first shot. I squeezed. The buck jumped forward, toward us by about five yards, and stood dead still. I thought I had hit him. Steve had flinched at the blast and wasn't sure what had happened. As I chambered another shell, the buck disappeared. Seconds later, Steve spotted him again, slowly moving uphill.

When the buck stopped again, I raised my hold slightly and fired. "You're low! Below his feet," Steve said. Again the buck was on the move. When he finally stopped, I held four feet above him and fired again, and again. "You're still low," was, all I heard. The buck topped the ridge and disappeared over it, pausing just long enough for Steve to gasp at the antler structure. Meanwhile, I desperately tried to reload.

We spent the next two hours trying to find blood, tracks, or any sign of the deer, but to no avail. On the ride home, we tried to assess the situation. We decided that my first shot must have been barely low; it probably sprayed the deer's back with rocks or brush on impact. My last shot was at least 200 yards longer than my first shot. But, the season was young and there were plenty of does around. We hoped we could find the buck again. I was definitely after only one deer.

We had planned to skip the next day, but the thought of that buck was more than I could take. I called Steve that night and he was ready to go. My 12-year-old son went along the next day. He watched with his mouth open as a high-90 to low-100 point buck lay down about 500 yards away. He was a nice 3-point (actually an 8-point by eastern count). Arizonans have a funny habit of ignoring the first point on any deer, calling it an "eye guard." In many cases, that's the biggest point on a Coues' deer. At any rate, my buck was not to be seen on that day, or on the next three hunting days I had over the next week-and-a-half. With each day, I learned more about the country. Occasionally I spotted some large tracks that I hoped were his, but I really believed that they were made by a passing mule deer.

In the meantime, word had gotten out that I had missed a huge, non-typical whitetail. Luckily, no one else was hunting the area, since the country really doesn't look like typical whitetail country. My dad had gotten a nice buck that scored about 97. He had over-estimated it in the field, mostly due to foggy conditions. But that had me convinced that "my" buck wasn't as big as I had first thought.

By 7:15 Christmas Eve morning, Steve and I were heading back to our vantage point. Two deer were working the hillside to the right of the rocky outcropping. I set up the spotting scope and looked. It was HIM! In our earlier confrontation he had been to the left of the outcrop. The previous outings had served as an education. I felt that I could make a stalk this time.

We dropped down to our left and, in minutes, we were completely out of any sightline to the deer, who were about 500 yards away. The doe was feeding, and the rut had begun. The buck couldn't take his eyes off the doe. We moved along quickly and quietly, Steve staying about 30 yards behind. If anyone was going to blow it, Steve was making sure it would be me. As I approached the outcrop, I eased up behind a small cedar tree. I couldn't see the deer or find the right spot. I backed off and moved further up the

ridge. As I moved to the edge again, I reached down for my field glasses and eased them up to my eyes. They came to focus right on the buck. He was about 200 yards out, still watching the doe. I put my hand down and Steve stopped, recognizing my signal.

I had nowhere to take a rest. I couldn't risk another move until both deer were out of sight again in the brush. Finally, they moved and so did I. I found an open spot behind a huge juniper tree and sat down, exposing just enough of myself so that I could see clearly. Another doe appeared from above, walking downhill toward the other two. I breathed a sigh of relief that she had not seen me, even though I never knew she was there.

When the doe disappeared, I stood and positioned myself behind a chest-high rock. I decided to start glassing with my scope instead of my binoculars. As I patiently watched, the first doe moved from behind a giant patch of prickly pear. As she did, the buck stepped into view, slightly quartering away from me. I positioned the cross hairs right behind his right shoulder and squeezed.

This time, there was no doubt. I recovered from the recoil in time to see the buck somersault down the hill and land under a big cedar tree. Steve was at my side in seconds. I held the gun, with the scope fixed on the tree where I'd last seen the buck. I had been shooting across a shallow ravine. As we moved toward the deer, I could see the spot clearly until we bottomed-out. From then on we hurried until we came to the big patch of prickly pear. From there, we circled around for what seemed like minutes, although I'm sure it was only seconds until I spotted the back of one huge antler in the brush beneath the cedar tree.

As Steve and I hauled the buck from beneath the tree, I was completely amazed. I had never dared to imagine that the buck was actually that big. The big tracks we had seen were his. His front feet were as big as a good mule deer. I guessed his score to be about 135, non-typical. He weighed 117 pounds. By Boone and Crockett standards, he had nine measurable points on his right antler and seven on his left. He was very heavily palmated and webbed, unlike any pictures I had ever seen. A 2-3/4 inch drop point was on his right antler, and his left antler sported a forked point that stuck straight out to the side.

I thoroughly enjoyed the next few hours. Dressing the buck and dragging him out was a pleasure. The following morning (Christmas), we green scored him at 137-7/8. Two-and-a half months later, Mike Cupell scored him for entry in B&C's Records Program. The 20th Big Game Awards Judges Panel officially measured the buck with a score of 134-2/8 points.

That beautiful buck was definitely a trophy hunter's dream, not taken strictly by chance, but with a measure of persistence and patience. He was my buck-of-a-lifetime.

Magic Moment

L. Victor Clark

Wyoming Mule Deer | Current Rank #37

IN THE EARLY 70S I STARTED HUNTING MULE DEER IN THE PINE
Forest Range located in northern Nevada. Starting in 1973,
every year for 20 years my wife Margie and I would spend our
vacation time camping, hunting, and fishing in this beautiful
place. And each year my obsession grew for big bucks. | CIRCA
I would pester Jim Jeffers, the biologist for that area of | *1992*
Nevada, always asking if he had observed any 40-inch bucks
during his aerial surveys. He would say that I was crazy, and
tell me that he only had seen a couple in his 20-plus years of
surveys. Pursuing anything that could help me find big bucks, I
researched everything that would tell me what it took to produce
monster mule deer: genetics, age, habitat, the best states and
where in those states to hunt.

My pursuits have led on hunting adventures into the Fifty
Mile Bench of Utah, the Kaibab Plateau along the Grand Canyon
in Arizona, Bass Hill in California, Unit 44 in Colorado, Steen's
Mountains in Oregon, Navaho Indian Reservation in Arizona, Rio
Arriba County in New Mexico, and Tin Cup Creek in Idaho. After

20 years of hunting these states I finally went to Wyoming in pursuit of my dream for a Boone and Crockett buck.

It was September 1992 when I ventured into the mule deer hideouts of Wyoming. Showing the way was a good friend, Frank Gonzales. Frank and I worked together for several years and shared a passion for hunting. Frank had hunted Wyoming and told me that he knew a spot where we would find big bucks. Frank was the only person I knew that would backpack, eat freeze-dried dinners, and sleep on the ground for several nights to experience the magical moment when those massive, wide antlers appear in the spotting scope and cast their spell—a spell that infects and enslaves the hunter to a lifelong pursuit of big bucks. After a 12-hour drive, we slept at the trailhead the first night. With guns, optics, sleeping bags, tent, food, clothes, and rain gear, we were on our way the next morning. We started into a drainage that led to one of the most rewarding hunts of my life. Both of us shouldered packs approaching 75 pounds. We cruised up the trail for the first couple miles fueled by the cold, crisp mountain air filling our lungs while the reds and yellows of autumn filled our eyes. I knew that one of those stringers of timber in the lofty rocky basins held a buck that appeared in every big buck hunter's dreams.

The deer season had been open for two days. As we hiked deeper into this enticing drainage, much to our dismay, we started to run into horse hunters returning to the trailhead with some very nice bucks. One hunter stopped to show off an awesome 32-inch, 5x7, which I must confess, made me envious. The further we went, the more hunters we encountered.

Fed up with all the horse hunters, Frank and I decided to leave the trail and follow a ridge to the top of a huge mountain. We climbed for eight hours with our overweight packs; when darkness fell, we had scaled only three quarters of the mountain. Finding a place flat enough to roll out a sleeping bag was not possible on the steep mountainside, so using a broken branch as a shovel, we scraped out enough of a flat spot for our sleeping bags. Leaving the trail and creek with only two quarts of water each, and the weather being unseasonably warm with temperatures in the 70s, we decided to save the water for drinking and skip the freeze-dried dinners. Exhausted and hungry, I drifted in a restless sleep where I chased big bucks all night.

Daybreak was clear and warm. The excitement of this new place and the potential of finding big bucks made the final ascent to the top go by quickly. We were counting on the northern exposure of one of these high alpine basins holding a small pond of snow melt to fill our canteens. The drought and unseasonably warm September dried up all those hopes. With a quart of water and a Power Bar in the last 30 hours, we worked our way along the backbone of the best big buck country I had ever hunted. After several hours of glassing our way through this new and beautiful place, I noticed that I had lost my scope covers. I told Frank that I was going to back track and look for them.

I returned unsuccessful to find Frank watching a huge 4-point bedded a half-mile away under a lone pine tree in one of the steepest rock chutes anywhere. Above the buck on top of a craggy ridge was a large Rocky Mountain goat guarding the buck's back door. It took several hours to circle around and come up above the buck's bed. When we dropped our packs for the final stalk, I told Frank to take the buck since he was the one who found him. Frank replied, "We will see how things play out."

Cresting the ridge only to find the goat and the buck gone proved to be a very depressing moment. After a few seconds of frantic searching I found the buck standing on the edge of a stand of heavy timber about 200 yards below. Frank was 15 yards to my left. Whispering to Frank, "I said there he is, take him."

Frank replied, "You take him."

This went back and forth several times with the buck two steps from vanishing forever. Finally, Frank said, "You shoot. I do not have a good shot."

With a solid rest and a perfect squeeze, my .300 Weatherby Magnum sent a 180-grain Nosler ballistic tip, almost instantaneously

the report of the whack signaled a solid hit. A second later Frank fired, I turned and asked Frank why he had shot.

Frank replied, "I did not know how good he was hit."

After sliding down the steep chute to the buck I found myself in awe of the size of this magnificent trophy. I had been an official measurer for Boone and Crockett for several years, and I had not measured or even seen anything that came close to the quality and size of this buck.

After photos, we began skinning and boning the deer for the long pack out. While skinning we could tell the buck had been hit with both my shot and Frank's shot. Both were fatal hits. I tagged the buck since I shot first. By the time we had completed processing the buck, it was dark. After finishing the last of the water we decided we had no choice but to spend the night where we were. Once again the mountainside was so steep that scraping out a spot against a bush for our sleeping bags was the only way to keep from rolling down the steep slope. As darkness fell a full moon rose silhouetting the huge antlers which I had placed on top of a bush at the foot of my sleeping bag. Looking up at my buck's antlers positioned perfectly on top of that bush with the full moon filling the sky in the back round is a memory that is still as vivid as if it happened last night.

Dawn broke on the third day finding us out of water. Being severely dehydrated and almost spent, we headed for the trailhead. Our overweight packs carried the additional load of a boned-out deer along with the cape and antlers. The weight of Frank's pack compounded by the steep decent drove Frank's toenails into the front of his boots and hobbled his progress. In the days and weeks to follow his toe nails turned black and fell off. There's no substitute for good boots!

It was about noon before we reached the bottom, and still, we were a half-mile from the trail and creek. My throat felt as if it would swell shut and my head was spinning. The temperature was in the 70s. Leaving Frank with the meat in the shade of a tree to nurse his toes, I took the canteens and made for the creek. Cold water has never tasted so good! Until I started to swallow, my throat was so dry that my first swallow stung and burned to the point that the pain brought tears to my eyes. I returned with full canteens and after a short rest Frank and I made it to the trailhead by late afternoon.

After a steak dinner and a good night's sleep, we started the drive home, but not without a quick stop in Afton where I bought a quarter-inch steel tape and rough-scored the buck at 209 inches with a greatest spread of 29-7/8 inches. I told Frank that there had not been a typical mule deer shot that scored that much in the last decade, and it truly was a world-class mule deer.

On the drive home I said, "Frank, if you had known that this deer was as tremendous as it is, would you have given me the first shot?"

He replied with a smile, "Yes, it means more to you than it does to me."

I continue to seek that magic moment that pulls me into the chase every fall. Though I have hunted for the big bucks every year, I have not been able to find the quality of the hunt or a trophy that comes close to the adventure Frank and I had in 1992. I have not shot a deer since—and probably will never shoot another one—but I will always hunt for that magic moment.

The Best Present

John R. Johnson

Alaska-Yukon Moose | Current Rank #11

As told by Doug Johnson (pictured at left)...

MY DAD AND I BOARDED A PLANE IN PORTLAND, OREGON, ON August 27, headed for Dillingham, Alaska. This was the beginning of a 10-day hunting trip for moose and caribou, in the Wood-Tikchik State Park. I graduated from Eastern Oregon State College in the spring of 1995.

CIRCA **1995**

Instead of giving me a gift with only monetary value, my dad decided to give me a gift that would be loaded with memories. This gift was a self-guided hunting trip in Alaska. We agreed that I would hunt for caribou and he would hunt for moose. This would be our first, but not the last hunting trip to Alaska.

In preparation for the trip, we had to buy a lot of reliable gear. This gear included just about everything you could think of that was waterproof, from the tent down to our apparel. Tom Slago, who owns and operates Bay Air with his wife, would be our air taxi for this trip. He told us to be prepared for rain, and that we would need trustworthy equipment.

We arrived in Dillingham the evening of the 27th. The sun was going to be up until 10 o'clock, so we were able to fly out to camp that evening. Tom used his Beaver with floats to fly us in. After a short flight, he dropped us at a small lake, with only a number for a name. We set up our tent and did the other necessary things that needed done around camp. There was nothing but lichen, moss, little patches of alders, rolling hills and caribou within sight of our tent. This looked to be the makings of a great hunt.

Moose season did not start until September 1, so I would be going after caribou first. After getting all the camp chores done, we decided to go for a look around. We had walked only 100 yards when we ran into two young bears, that bolted after catching our scent. This was the first time I had seen a grizzly bear, and after all the stories I heard and read, it was nice to see they headed in the other direction. After this encounter, we hiked up to one of the many rolling hills to get a better look at the surroundings. It was getting late in the evening, so there were a lot of caribou coming out of the brush. We saw close to a 100 caribou in a short amount of time, with many good bulls mixed in with cows. I could not shoot one until the next day because it is illegal to hunt game animals in Alaska on the same day you fly in.

We awoke the next morning to rainy and windy conditions, just right for caribou hunting. The wind blew away the pesky mosquitoes and gnats, allowing the caribou to stay out of the brush longer to feed. We left as the sun was coming up, and were only a couple hundred yards out of camp before we spotted the first band of caribou. There were a few bulls in the bunch, but nothing that impressed me. We continued hunting the rest of the morning, using our binoculars to find them, and a spotting scope to see if they were worth chasing. It was not until noon that I spotted the bull I wanted. There was only one problem; he was a mile away and standing on the other side of a brushy swamp. We guessed where he was going, since caribou never seem to stop moving, and took off to intercept him.

When we dropped down into the swampy lake bottom, we quickly lost sight of the bull. It took us well over a half an hour to cover one mile in the rough terrain, but we finally arrived at our destination. Dad and I could not locate the bull, so we started walking toward a little rise, thinking he had slipped behind it. We had taken no more than 10 steps, when he came crashing out of the brush, and through a creek, not 50 yards away. The bull came out on the far side of the creek bed, and made a fateful mistake by looking back. I shouldered my .300 Weatherby and sent a 180-grain bullet into his right shoulder. The hunt was over and the work began. There was not a tree to be found for miles to hang the meat, so we field dressed and skinned the animal. We left the meat on the hide until we could pack it out the next morning. I felt the bull, heavily beamed and tall, with nice tops, would score well. He would later score 380-5/8 points under the Boone and Crockett scoring system. This was not enough for an All-time listing, but was enough for the Award listing in *Boone and Crockett Club's 23rd Big Game Awards* book. We spent the next day packing out meat and enjoying the scenery.

The following day, Tom came and picked us up for our short flight to moose camp. Non-residents cannot hunt moose in the unit where we were, so we moved 20 miles toward Tikchik Lake. On our way over to the next camp we saw a lot of moose, including two nice bulls. We landed on another small lake with no name, and proceeded to set up camp. It was early in the day so we decided to go look for the bulls that we had seen from the air. From several hundred feet up, the terrain did not look to be very challenging, but when we started walking through the brush, we found it was very rough going. The alders were over 10-feet tall and laid over on their side. They then arched five feet up, toward the sun. This made a lot of areas impenetrable, causing many detours. Beaver dams also caused a lot of problems. Every stream flooded the surroundings because of these little critters. These beaver ponds were very deep and also caused detours and lost time. Fed up with trying to take the low road, we headed for the hills. We found that it was much easier going in the hilly country than down in the swampy bottoms.

When we got to the hilltop, near where we had seen the moose, we sat down and started to glass. It was a very warm and calm day, allowing the bugs to be out in full force, which pushed the moose back into the brush thickets. We searched the little valley below us and found the two moose we had seen from the air, and they were both legal to shoot when the season opened. At the time, non-residents had to shoot a moose with three brow tines on a side, or which had an outside spread greater than 50 inches. For two hunters who had seen only a few moose before, we decided to look for one that had three or more brow tines per side. When you consider how big a moose is, it was hard for us to tell how wide 50 inches really was.

On August 31, we awoke to a downpour and decided to stay inside the tent for the morning. The rain let up for a little in the afternoon, so we took an excursion to the north side of the lake and saw lots of caribou and moose tracks, but no animals. Most of the area to the north of camp was low country with no way of getting up high to look for moose. The area—easily accessed by connecting meadows—was not our lucky place to find a moose. We had heard that bulls would come down as breeding season progressed. This was only the very beginning of the rut, with the biggest bulls just beginning to rub their velvet, and the bulls had not yet moved to the low country.

That night, back at camp, I convinced my dad we needed to go back to where we had seen the moose the first day. He liked the easy walking country northeast of camp, but we did not see any animals there. My dad and I have experienced a lot of hunting and packing into the wilderness in the Minam country of eastern Oregon. I knew that if he shot anything three to four miles from camp we would have no problem retrieving it.

We awoke the following morning to partly sunny skies, and a quick breakfast of instant oatmeal and hot cider. With our fanny packs filled with the usual supplies of food, bug dope, and a first-aid kit, we set out with high hopes of finding a bull moose. Halfway into the valley, I spooked a bull with my noisy rain gear. It was not raining, but the dew on the grass and limbs was enough to soak you to the bone. We chased this little guy around for a couple of hours, but never did get a good look at him. We proceeded to the hilltop where we could look down on the valley. We arrived at the top around 11:30 A.M., and began glassing. Not seeing the bulls where they had been previously, we began searching elsewhere. We did see an exceptional caribou, bigger than the one I had taken, and I wished I still had my tag.

I decided to start looking a little closer in, since we had only been looking far out into the valley. Down below us, on a little shelf 200 yards away, I spotted a bull. He was hard to see because the brush was so tall. His antlers looked huge. Neither of us had taken a moose before and we did not know if the bull was legal. Dad readied his rifle, while I looked for brow tines. I could not tell through my binoculars, so we retrieved the spotting scope from my fanny pack. The scope had fogged up due to all the moisture and almost cost us Dad's bull. The bull did not know we were there, and kept nipping the tender new growth shoots off the alders. From our angle, I couldn't tell with my binoculars if he was legal. I needed a front view to be able to see his brow tines. About that time, he laid down in the big alder patch and all I could see were the tops of his antlers. It was now a waiting game.

While we were waiting, my dad had grown tired of the gnats that were biting at his skin and buzzing around his head, so he pulled out a stick of bug dope. He had just finished applying the repellent when the moose stood up, and looked right at us. The air currents had carried the nasty smell of the bug dope right to him. This, however, gave me enough time to see that he had at least four brow tines on each side. As the bull turned to run, I told my dad to shoot. My dad's 7mm roared and the bull did not even flinch. He shot again and nothing happened. As he prepared to shoot a third time, the bull stopped and looked back at us, allowing for one good shot. After the third shot, he was off to the races again, acting as if nothing was wrong. After winding through the alders, he stopped in a group of trees, more than 300 yards away. The bull stopped and hung his head in a small patch of trees. With a final shot to the neck, the hunt was over.

I scaled down the hill to find his trophy, while he stayed behind just in case the moose got back on his feet. After crossing a little stream and climbing up the other side, I located the patch of trees where we thought the bull would be. I approached with caution but there was no need. There before me was the biggest game animal I had ever seen. What a magnificent animal! Dad quickly came down from the knoll to claim his trophy. We both stood in awe and wondered how in the heck we were going to butcher this giant. After a big struggle to move the bull, it was time for pictures. Unfortunately, the camera jammed after the first photo. While setting up for the "one" picture, we realized how wide his antlers were. Stretching his rifle from the outside of one antler, to the opposite side, the gun only made it a little over half way. Using this as a gauge, we estimated that the bull had an outside spread of at least 72 inches. We thought this was big, but neither of us had any clue how big.

Having good backpacks was a real bonus when we realized that we would be packing 600 pounds of boned-out meat on our backs. It ended up taking us four days to get everything back to our camp. The most challenging part of the pack ended up being the antlers, and I got the job of hauling the monstrous rack back to camp. The easiest way would have been to split the bone between the antlers, but my dad did not want to risk voiding entry into the records book, if they scored well. All that water and brush got the last laugh. While covering the four miles back to camp, I bounced from one bush to the next, slipping and falling in frustration the whole way.

Tom picked us up on September 6, one day earlier than planned. This is when we really started to wonder how big my dad's bull was. Everyone who saw the rack was stopped and asked questions. Many of the people we talked to said that it was the biggest bull they had ever seen in all their years living in Alaska. We put a tape measure on the rack and found it to be close to 78-inches wide.

We promised that we would have the antlers scored when we got back to Oregon.

When we arrived back home, I had the rack green scored at 255-3/8 points. We still didn't know how big was big, so Dad had Buck Buckner score the rack after the necessary drying time. Buck taped the bull at 254-1/8 points. He called us the next day and said that it would rank approximately third in the world, if the score stood. Wow! What a moose for two guys who had only seen a few Alaska-Yukon moose before this trip. The bull was part of the 23rd Big Game Awards program and was officially verified with a score of 249-3/8 points.

My dad has since moved to Kodiak, Alaska, and took the antlers with him. They are now on display in the lobby at Kodiak Inn in Kodiak.

More than anything I will always cherish the memories and companionship I had with my dad on this trip. It was the best present I could have ever received for graduation. I will not look at this trip for the quality of trophies we were able to take—they were a bonus— rather, I will always remember the good time we had together.

Killing the Wind

Michael L. Ward

Alaska Brown Bear | Current Rank #13

I COULD NOT BELIEVE MY EYES. I DOUBLE-CHECKED AND IT REALLY was my name, and the address was correct. I was reading an Anchorage newspaper listing results of the recent drawing for Alaska permit hunts. I had just won a highly-coveted Kodiak brown bear permit in the best area for trophy bears, the southern end of Kodiak Island. This was July of 1998 and the hunt was for the following spring, over nine months away. I felt like a kid again waiting for the opening day of duck season.

CIRCA 1999

Another fortunate event occurred shortly thereafter when Dr. George Pappas from Denver called me. His son, a former co-worker of mine with the Alaska Department of Fish and Game in Dutch Harbor, told him about my bear permit. George loves bear hunting, particularly Kodiak Island. He asked me about my plans and who would accompany me. I told him my plans were not set but if he was interested in going, he was welcome to come along. Having hunted the same area six years previously, he was a wealth of information. He killed a huge bear with a 29-inch skull. His hunting story was published in the *Boone and Crockett Club's 22nd Big Game Awards* book. Additionally, his picture is included in the eleventh edition of *Records of North American Big Game*. Yes, George was interested in accompanying me. Over the months we made many phone calls formulating our plans. My permit allowed 15 continuous days of hunting between April 1 and May 15. We would arrive in Kodiak on Sunday evening April 25, then check in with Fish and Game and fly out to camp on Monday morning.

This was not going to be a backpack hunt. George and I planned to stay at least 17 days; consequently, we wanted a comfortable camp. Instead of my usual Super Cub flight, I chartered Peninsula Airlines Grumman Goose to fly us to camp. This is a large amphibious plane that can carry nearly a ton of gear. We would be fully loaded when we took off.

After an interminable wait, April 24 arrived. I left my homestead near Tok, Alaska, early for the five-hour drive to Anchorage where I would pick up George at the airport. We visited some friends and did some packing in preparation for our flight to Kodiak the next evening.

Winter ran late on Kodiak in 1999. Lakes remained frozen with lots of snow on the ground, not typical for late April. Advice to leave snowshoes behind proved a big mistake. I was unable to borrow a pair but did manage to purchase emergency shoes that pilots carry as part of their survival gear.

Monday morning dawned clear and calm. At 8 A.M. we checked into Fish and Game and then proceeded to the airport for our flight to camp. At 11 A.M. we took off on the hour flight south to a small bay. The day was gorgeous. Clear blue skies with snowy mountains of Kodiak Island and the Alaska Peninsula to the north and west, and calm blue waters of the North Pacific Ocean to the south and east. Rugged Kodiak Island was spectacular! There is nowhere as pretty as coastal Alaska on a clear day. We unloaded our gear and the plane was off. The rest of the day was spent setting up camp. Kodiak winds are notorious for shredding tents. We used George's eight-man dome tent, double or triple guying each of the numerous tie-off points.

Toward evening we spotted two people walking along the beach. As they neared our camp we greeted them. It was the guide who operates out of that area and a client. They were packing a bear hide taken the previous day. It was a large, well-furred male that green scored just short of the Boone and Crockett minimum. They had hunted hard for 13 days seeing few bear.

Sleep came hard to me that night; I was too excited. Red foxes were breeding and their screams could be heard throughout the night. Toward dawn the wind came up and by 8 A.M. it was blowing a gale. It was to be our constant companion for the rest of the hunt. Southern Kodiak Island is wide open, with treeless wind-swept rolling hills and a spine of mountains. We ate a good breakfast and were out early. A long day of hunting produced a sighting of one bear at long range. The wind was fierce, at least 70 knots. We hid from it most of the day, spending long hours glassing.

The second day was pretty much a repeat of the first, very strong winds making hunting difficult. A sow and two cubs were spotted at long range. The snow line was at about 900 feet and very few tracks were visible. It appeared few bears were out of their dens yet. This would correspond to what the previous hunters had seen.

We decided to change tactics the next day. We would hunt up in the mountains in the area George had taken his bear. The wind had switched directions and was now out of the west, again at a fierce 70 knots. We followed an old bear trail used for many years and by noon we arrived at a good vantage point just below snowline to glass for the rest of the day. We hid behind car-size boulders daring to stick our head up into the raging wind to glass as long as we could stand it. I cannot overstate how fierce the winds were. After about three hours George looked up, and on the mountain right above us about 1,000 feet was a bear digging roots. We sized him up and decided he was very large and un-rubbed with long hair blowing in the wind. I decided to circle back downwind and climb up to him. A large boulder was my goal. It would shelter me from his view during the half-hour stalk and allow me a good rest for a shot at about 100 yards. The harsh wind was now my ally; it remained constantly in my face.

The bear was intent on digging out something and he was not looking around. Climbing the steep mountain was fatiguing. As I closed to within ten feet of the boulder I felt the wind on the back of my neck for just an instant. I ran to the boulder, peeked around, and was horrified to see the bear, with his nose up, moving away. After over three hours of constant wind, I had been betrayed. He was speeding up as I chambered a round and I quickly threw a shot at him as he disappeared around the mountain. It was a foolish off-hand shot. I was tired and unsteady. After over an hour of searching his tracks in the snow I was relieved to find no blood. A fortunate miss, as a wounded bear traveling long distance would have been the most likely result if I hit him with a bad shot. I was also very sad. It was a very large bear with a beautiful hide. I was afraid it would be my only chance at a great bear.

We glassed a few more hours before returning to camp. A delicious lamb chop dinner livened my spirits. Hunting conditions may be harsh, but at least we were eating well—no freeze-dried food on this trip.

The next morning we arose early and headed north to hunt a large valley that looked like good bear habitat. The valley was ringed by steep snow covered mountains that would provide good denning areas. Very few bear trails could be seen in the snow, however. A creek meandered through the valley floor, terminating in an estuary at salt water. This would provide good early season food in the form of grass and roots. Winter-killed deer could be found on the flats. We glassed from a knob most of the day. The west wind was still howling. I literally threw myself to the ground to keep from being blown down the hill. A young bear that spent about an hour roaming the flats was spotted early. It was fun to watch, and encouraged us. Spring bear hunting on Kodiak Island involves long hours of patient glassing. This is the breeding season. Large males roam widely in their search for a mate. Winter snow has knocked down the luxuriant summer vegetation allowing excellent glassing over expansive terrain. We did spot another medium-sized bear before returning to camp for dinner, after which I climbed into the hills behind camp and glassed the flats to the south. The hills trailed off to the ocean about two miles away. A few deer, survivors of the hard winter, and a fox kept me entertained until dark.

We were on the same knob enduring the same raging west wind on the fifth day. George quickly spotted two bears, one chasing another, far to the south near the ocean. This is the area where the previous hunter took his bear. These bears appeared to be a large male chasing a female. They soon moved out of sight heading up into the foothills. Shortly I spotted another bear, nose down like a bird dog, following their trail. This bear also quickly moved out of sight. This was very encouraging. Bear were becoming more abundant as the hunt progressed. After a few more hours of glassing we returned to camp for lunch. I decided to hunt up in the hills where the bears headed while George remained to work around camp. Toward evening I spotted two bears, presumably the same courting couple, near where we had last seen them. The third bear was not seen. Possibly there was a fight and one was run off. They were moving slowly, allowing me to approach to about 500 yards. The larger bear appeared to be a medium-size male that was rubbed. They slowly moved out of sight over about an hour while I enjoyed watching them. The smaller, presumably female, bear would not allow the larger bear to get close to her. Returning to camp at dark I was again treated to one of George's lamb dinners. We discussed the next day's hunt and decided on the area where the previous hunter made his kill.

There was a diminishment in the wind that evening, still a gale from the west but only about 40 knots. We hiked south about two miles to a small range of hills where we spent much of the day glassing from the highest point. Remains of the previous kill could be seen. Eagles and a fox took turns feeding on the meager remnants of what a week previously must have been close to half a ton of brown bear carcass.

The gray whale migration was now in full swing around Kodiak Island. From our vantage point we would see three or four whales an hour swimming past on their way north to summer in the Bering Sea and Arctic Ocean. I was getting drowsy in the mid-day sun when all of a sudden George said, "There's a bear."

About 400 yards away stood an enormous bear. He was absolutely huge, with a belly to match. He was pestering a female that would not let him get near her. She was much more aggressive toward him than the female I observed the previous day. He cornered her at the edge of a 100-foot cliff with jagged rocks below where she whirled on him, snapping at his face, and then agilely eluded him. He stood over twice her height and was also completely rubbed; no trophy here, except for the potential World's Record skull. I decided not to take him. This hurt George. He really wanted me to get this bear. The two quickly moved off. We attempted to follow, but never did see them again.

We returned to camp for an early dinner and then hunted behind camp until dark. No more bears were seen that day. We discussed the next day's hunt and decided to climb into the mountains again.

The next day the wind conditions kept us from going to the mountains we planned to hunt. We didn't see a bear the entire day and were starting to feel a little discouraged.

A big break came during the night when the wind switched around to a west wind. This allowed us to hunt the area we considered most productive—the mountain where George killed his bear and I missed a bear. A big breakfast of bacon and eggs started our day. We were then off on the three-hour climb into the mountains. A comparatively calm 50-knot wind blew into our faces. We posted ourselves on a rock affording the best visibility and settled in for a long day of glassing. In early afternoon George spotted a good-sized bear below us, probably about a nine-footer, moving along slowly at 300 yards. George strongly recommended I quickly go down and kill it. I looked it over. He was obviously rubbed. George reminded me we were running out of time and not seeing many bears.

"I'd rather go home without a bear than kill one I would not be proud of," was my reply.

"That may well be the case," was his.

The next morning we rode out a biting sleet storm and stayed in camp to set up another dome tent. We did hunt close to camp in the afternoon, but no bears were spotted.

The wind gradually switched around to a north wind during the night. We decided another try in the mountains was in order. We took our customary promontory to glass from throughout the day. In early afternoon I decided to take a hike and look over some country to the south. After a couple hours I returned and continued to glass with George. All of a sudden he spotted a bear. It was on the mountain across a narrow pass from us. I looked up in time to see it stand, stretch, yawn, and then lay back down. I got a good look at the hair on its back and side blowing in the wind. He was not rubbed, and a good-sized bear. He was lying on a bench high up on a steep mountainside above us about 250 yards away. It seemed tired and we felt it had just emerged from its den. We wanted to get closer but to do so meant dropping down off our mountain into the pass. My only shot was to shoot from where we were. He was lying lengthwise to us with only his head and shoulder tops visible. He looked small through my scope. The wind was also roaring out of the north crosswise to us at about 50 knots, a very difficult shot. I set up a padded rest and waited, planning to shoot when he stood.

After about 45 minutes I was getting cold. Temperatures were in the high 30s and I was exposed to the wind. I was afraid I would start shivering and miss my shot. About every five minutes the wind would stop for 5 or 10 seconds. I told George my predicament and that I planned to shoot during the next lull. We got ready. Sure enough the wind stopped a couple of minutes later, at which point I said, "Here we go, George" and fired. It was a hit. Just when I thought he was finished he arose and staggered off behind a rock, apparently dying. I now had the formidable task of climbing up a snow chute and skinning out the bear. This would obviously be an individual effort as I would not ask George to attempt the climb. I was crossing the pass to assess the situation when suddenly the bear appeared, staggering through the snow, obviously hit hard. He was crossing in front of me at about 50 yards as I fired twice more at his lungs. Down he went for the final time. As I approached I had the feeling that he looked rather small. I poked his rump repeatedly with the muzzle of my rifle, then in the eye. There was no movement. Still, I was afraid to touch him. He wasn't small anymore, but I finally mustered up the courage to touch him. His hide was the most luxurious I had ever felt. His claws were white and his head was massive. He was flawless, a perfect bear. I said a prayer of thanks to God for allowing me to kill such a magnificent animal.

George waded across the thigh-deep snow and after a few minutes of joyous backslapping and admiring the bear we decided pictures were in order. It was now 6 o'clock, not enough time for us to skin out the bear and return to camp. We rolled it onto its back. I worried the thick hide and huge body would insulate it from the snow and keep it from cooling down. I decided to skin open the belly and down the sides to allow it to cool as best it could. I left some stinky socks near the bear and relieved myself around it in the hope of discouraging any scavengers.

I awoke the next morning to beautiful, calm blue skies. It was as if killing the bear also killed the wind. For the first time in 12 days it was pleasant to be out. I left camp with my pack and skinning gear. George loaned me his .44 Magnum revolver to carry in place of my rifle. The farther I walked into the hills the more I regretted that decision. I felt nervous walking those hills in the presence of large bears without a rifle, especially as I neared the kill, which a bear may have been claiming.

Once I finally had the hide off I was even more in awe of the bear. What a physical specimen! Not fat as you think of a large bear. It was all massive muscle. There were some puncture wounds in one leg that were festering, probably from a fight the previous fall. The neck was nearly three feet in circumference. It took me seven hours to finish the skinning chores and I was tuckered out. I tried to load the hide and head back to camp, but kept bogged down in the deep snow. I would have to return the next day with more cord and my snowshoes. I returned to camp with only the head. George was amazed when he saw it. His bear scored high in the Boone and Crockett book and he said this one was bigger. We did a very rough measurement without calipers of about 12 inches by 19 inches or 31 inches, which was larger than the current number one bear. I was excited but worried as I still had an unprotected bear hide in the hills to pack out. I gathered up my snowshoes and the cord I needed to attach it to my pack the next day.

After a long struggle I finally got the hide back to camp. The stretched measurement was 11 feet claw-to-claw, and 9 feet nose-to-tail for a squared size of 10 feet. I added 50 pounds of salt to the hide, and covered it with a tarp to keep off the light rain while we waited the last two days for our trip back to Anchorage.

After our plane ride back we checked into a hotel and cleaned up before heading to Alaska Department of Fish and Game (ADFG) for the mandatory check out. When John Crye at ADFG office saw my bear he said, "This may be the one we've been looking for."

A few years previously, a very large bear was tranquilized, sampled, measured, and a number tattooed in its lips. A very rough measurement of the skull with, of course, the hide still attached indicated that it was larger than the current number one bear. John proceeded to measure my bear. While not the big one, it still was the fifth largest bear sealed by ADFG since they started record keeping in 1954. John also discovered that my bear had also been sampled, as he found a number tattooed in the lips. A year later I received a letter from him telling me that the premolar tooth he extracted was sectioned and found to be 12 years old.

I will always wonder if the huge bear we saw was the big one, a new world's record. Body wise, he was substantially bigger than my bear. Still, I would not trade my bear with its flawless hide for the world's record skull.

Emotional High

Mary A. Isbell

Idaho Shiras' Moose | Current Rank #17

HUNTING HAS ALWAYS BEEN A VERY IMPORTANT ACTIVITY FOR OUR family. My Grandpa Isbell taught my dad how to hunt and the tradition has continued through the generations. Our family consists of my mom, dad, and four daughters. I'm the youngest of the girls. Dad started each of us shooting when we were about five years old with .22s and used various firearms working up to a bolt action, scoped .22 long rifle. We've all spent countless hours practicing shooting. Once we reached ten years of age, we started with hunting rifles. We all started with the same .243 and then progressed on to our .270s and .30-06 rifles. Shooting isn't all; we just love the outdoors and the wildlife. We ride our horses, hike, study animals, and then when we're home, we pour over books and videos.

CIRCA 2000

The hunt for my moose took place when I was 12 years old. Even though this was the first trip I was the hunter, I'd been going for years when my sisters and dad were hunting. I've hiked with them over some of the most difficult country in southeastern Idaho that you could imagine. My dad loves the steepest, roughest, and rockiest mountains he can find. My sisters and I have given them names like "Death Mountain," "Heart Attack Hill," or "Heart-stroke Mountain." I actually shouldn't complain, though, because we've been very successful in finding our game.

In Idaho each hunter can apply for special controlled permits for hunting. If you apply for moose, sheep, or goat then you can't apply for special deer, antelope, or elk permits. Each year seems to be a ritual in deciding what each of us wants to apply for. My quest for moose actually began in late summer 1999. On a late August morning, my dad and one of my sisters had gone on an early morning hike while the rest of us stayed at our cabin. When they returned, my dad was almost speechless. He claimed that he had seen a moose bedded about a mile away that appeared to be a top-end, B&C-class animal. They had hiked down reasonably close to the animal and studied it through the binoculars. As I listened to the excitement in their voices, I could tell that this one must be very special. Dad's very objective and knowledgeable about evaluating trophy game and doesn't usually get as easily excited as he was this time. Right then and there it was decided that all of us would apply for moose, hoping that someone could draw a permit while this special animal was still alive. None of us had drawn in 1999, but one of our close friends did. She took a gorgeous bull, but it wasn't the one that Dad had seen.

As the year 2000 approached, we did the traditional application scheme. We'd check on the Internet each evening until the results were posted. When the results were out, we couldn't believe it. Even though drawing odds are low, my older sister Becky and I, along with our close friend Craig Heiner, had drawn! The quest for the giant moose began.

It was traditional in our family that I would use my grandpa Isbell's .30-06 for the hunt. It is a Model 70 Winchester that he bought in 1945. My dad had a custom stock made for it in 1982 and had developed some handloads with 165-grain Nosler Partition bullets. It shoots very well and my older sisters had taken great game with it including impressive Shiras' moose. Dad had me practice all summer with the rifle in anticipation of the hunt. My sister, Becky, would also use the rifle since it wouldn't be likely to have us both see two great bulls together at the same time.

Summer is a hard time to find trophy bull moose. They are in the thick timber bedded during most of the day and we didn't see very many large bulls on our scouting trips. We did spend a lot of time scouting by hiking, by horseback, and by riding in the pickup. About two weeks before the hunt, our friend, Bob Hudman called. He could hardly speak. When he started telling us about the moose, I could tell it was the one we had hoped to find again. I could get a good impression of the size of the animal by listening to my dad and his friends. When they seem uncontrollably nervous, then I know it's special. As he described this great animal and its location, we decided that we'd all try to keep an eye on him until opening day in August. We tried to keep track of the animal, but he seemed to disappear a few days before the hunt. We were afraid that something had happened to him or that he'd just left the country. Even though we hadn't seen the moose for four or five days, opening day was a must. After some discussion, it was decided that I'd have the opportunity on opening day and my parents arranged for me to miss school. I must thank our dear friend Craig Heiner. He was present and helped on the hunt, and didn't even bring his rifle so that it would be my day.

We all met at Hudman's cabin near the Tex Creek Wildlife Management Area on opening morning. Our group included my mom and dad, Bob, Sandy, and Charity Hudman, and Craig and Debbie Heiner. This was one big moose expedition. We traveled by ATVs to a place where we could glass. It wasn't 30 minutes until the monster was spotted. He was back in the exact spot where Bob had seen him two weeks earlier. We immediately maneuvered in front of him, but couldn't get a shot. We watched him through binoculars as he went into the next canyon and into an aspen stand. Then we crept over the ridge above him and I prepared for the shot. The wind was howling, blowing a light drizzle of rain and the range

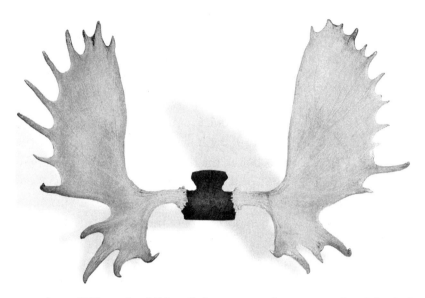

was about 250 yards. All in all, it was a perfect moose day. My dad got me set up on a large rock. Bob and Craig were using separate video cameras so we'd be sure to record the event. The rifle seemed to jump around uncontrollably with the wind and the pounding of my heart. It seemed like a long time, but my dad told me to wait until there was a break in the wind and then take the shot. When the wind slowed, I carefully pulled the trigger. Immediately after the shot, Bob exclaimed, "You got him! You don't realize how big of a moose you just shot! He's going high in the records book!"

This really got me shaking. All of a sudden the moose stood up again, Dad and Bob both told me to hit him again. As I squeezed the trigger for the second shot the bull went down for good just as the shot went off. The next few minutes were pure chaos. My dad, Bob, Craig, and Sandy were all acting almost crazy with the excitement of this great animal. They hiked down to the moose first, leaving Dad and me on the ridge in case the moose got up.

As my dad and I hiked down to him, I could still hear Craig almost screaming what a monster he was. He was everything we'd imagined and more. Bob and Sandy went to get the remainder of the crowd. Dad, Craig, and I simply marveled at the size of the animal. Not only were his antlers huge, but his body was immense. We all discussed this, and later when the carcass was weighed at the meat processor, they confirmed how big he was.

After the photo session, I really learned how big a large moose is. With all eight of us helping, it was a real chore to take care of and pack out a large animal like that. When we checked my moose in at the Idaho Department of Fish and Game the excitement rose again. It was a continuous emotional high.

Our moose hunting didn't end that day. For the next two months we hunted every Saturday, several weekdays and after school for my sister Becky's and Craig's moose. We spent those days hiking, riding, and checking out several big bull moose. There are many unique stories about those two other great bulls like the day my sister got hypothermia, but that's another story. They both did get their trophy animals near the end of the season.

After getting this bull, we took him to one of the premier taxidermists in the west, Jay Ogden, in Richfield, Utah. Even though he's mounted some amazing trophy animals, he was excited about the opportunity to mount this magnificent specimen and will create a mount that compliments my trophy. We have already chosen a spot in our home for him.

I'll probably never take another animal as large for its species as my first bull moose. This day will be with me forever; the memory of the hunt, the family and friends, and the privilege to be in the great outdoors hunting.

Our Lucky Hunt

Kyle Lopez

Colorado Mule Deer | Current Rank #12

B<i>eep, Beep, Beep!</i> The alarm went off, signaling that my hunting season had finally arrived. I rolled over to my nightstand and silenced the alarm, then jumped out of bed. To no surprise, my dad was already up and ready, along with my uncle. I grabbed some breakfast and began to get ready too. I had to make sure I had all my gear—rifle, knife, camo clothing, and, of course, my orange. When we were ready, I ran out to the truck and we were off. It took about 35 minutes traveling in the dark to get to our hunting area.

CIRCA
2007

On the first day we chose to go to a more popular area to see how many hunters were out in the unit. After a long and hard day of hunting, I came home empty-handed. However my uncle harvested a great buck, which Dad green scored at 194. We hunted hard the next day, including a trip into the area where I would eventually take my trophy. On this first trip into the area I missed a great buck and once again came home empty-handed.

The next morning I had to go to school. I was still feeling frustrated and thinking about the buck I had missed. I was not able to hunt the next evening because of an after-school appointment to turn in football gear. That turned out to be an even more frustrating day; all I could think about was the buck that I had missed.

We were not able to hunt for the next two days, but finally on November 7, 2007, Dad and I were both able to take off early one day. Dad said he had a gut feeling that it would be our lucky hunt. We decided to make a trip back into the area where I had missed. However, we had a different plan of attack this time. We quickly and quietly maneuvered our way up a deep creek bottom surrounded by steep hillsides on both sides, weaving in and out through the tangled maze of burned timber to the base of the mountain.

It was a good three-mile hike. As we started to top out at the head of the creek, the hillsides became more visible. Dad paused for a moment and pulled up his glasses to look ahead while we still had the cover of the creek. He quietly whispered that there were two young does up ahead. I looked at them through my binoculars to make sure they were does as well. I just couldn't draw antlers on either of them. So we snuck around to their left. As we did, the does spotted us. We paused for a moment to see what they were going to do. The excitement was starting to build. Just the sight of those deer and how close we were to them made it feel as if we had stepped into their bedroom.

In that moment we were struck with luck. The does curiously started walking toward us. As we held our position, I could only wonder what was going to happen next. *Would the does finally realize what we were and blow out of the country, taking the rest of the forest life with them? Or would we be able to trick them and slip past to continue our quest for a buck?* They paused about 50 yards from us, discovered that we weren't deer and quietly trotted off. They left in the direction from where they had come, which worked in our favor. Dad's plan was to move away from them and toward a steep hillside that had lush, green vegetation on it.

As we turned to start toward the hillside, Dad stopped and looked ahead again. He said, "Kyle, there is a buck looking right at us." As Dad was looking through his glasses he told me it was definitely a mature buck worth shooting. Dad was standing next to a burned tree, and as he stepped around it, he told me to rest my rifle against the side of the tree to take the shot. As I got my first look at the buck through the scope, it appeared to be just what Dad had said. He was facing us, looking in our direction with an intense stare.

I steadied my breathing, let out my breath, held it, and squeezed the trigger—Pow! The buck jumped a mile high as the shot went off. As he turned in mid-air, his head immediately hit the ground, and like a bulldozer, he plowed his way over a small bluff. He collapsed out of sight. Dad exclaimed, "You got him Kyle, good job!"

We hugged as Dad's gut feeling about me getting a deer that evening came true. We gave the buck a little time (what seemed like hours) before we went to find him. The adrenaline was definitely flowing and the excitement welled inside me. Dad told me to get another round ready as we took off to go track him. When we arrived at the spot where we last saw the buck standing, we immediately found blood and tracked him about 50 feet. He was in a small ditch. As we were approaching him, it looked like he had fallen into an old dead bush. My dad told me to get my gun ready. My heart was pumping. I could see the grey color of his body as Dad picked up a rock and tossed it toward the buck's belly. As the rock hit and bounced off the buck's body, Dad said, "He's done, Kyle."

That is when our luck took an enormous turn for the better. As I was securing my rifle, I heard my dad say, "Oh my God." He just kept saying, "Oh my God, Oh my God," over and over.

Neither one of us was prepared for what we found lying at our feet. We assumed I had shot a good buck, but never in our wildest dreams thought it was that tremendous. As I stood next to my dad, looking at the buck, there were so many points coming off his antlers, it looked as if the bush that he had fallen into had overtaken him. His antlers were heavy; it seemed as if there were hundreds of points going in all different directions. From that point on, there would be no words to describe the buck—at least not that anyone would believe without seeing it with their own eyes.

Dad gave me a big hug. We had several high fives before we dressed out my deer and got him ready for the journey back to the truck. Dad had decided to drag the buck out; we were losing light, making it too difficult to quarter the deer. What should have been an hour-long pack-out turned into a four-hour ordeal through a creek bed knotted with twisted, fallen, burned timber. It seemed as if we would drag for a hundred yards then clear debris for a hundred yards. Finally, we made it to the truck and loaded up my deer. We had done it, and now everything was over—so I thought.

Not too long after killing my deer, the phone calls and e-mails began pouring in. It first started with offers to write magazine articles for such publications as *Eastman's, Hunting Illustrated, Muley Crazy,* and *Trophy Hunter.* Greg Merriam wrote many of these articles. Then it escalated into offers to attend and present my deer at the various hunting shows. That's when I got a phone call from the man who made most of this possible, Roger Selner.

There is just no way to explain the excitement and emotion over what we were looking at that day. I am very proud of myself and what I accomplished. I would like to thank the entire Eastman family for all their support, King's Outdoor World for its article and calendars, Mel Siefke at Wildlife Recapture Taxidermy, and Greg Merriam for the articles he has written. However the two most important people I would like to thank are Roger Selner and my dad.

As Luck Would Have It

Carla A. de Kock

Northwest Territories Musk Ox | Current Rank #12

IN THE NORTHWEST TERRITORIES, CANADA, THERE IS A MUSK ox draw system in place. Applications are submitted in May, and the draw is held each year before June 1. Tags are not awarded to anyone who has received a tag for any of the previous four seasons. Hunting season lasts over eight months beginning in August 1 and running through April 15.

CIRCA **2012**

As my luck had it, I was drawn and the adventure began. My first adventure took place in September 2011. My guide (and spouse) Mark Caswell and I flew from Yellowknife, Northwest Territories to Norman Wells, Northwest Territories. Once there, we flew in by helicopter to the Norman Range just outside of Norman Wells, and visibility was low due to fog in the mountains. We landed and set up camp at the best available location. It turns out we were in for a lot of work hiking for our hunt. We hunted hard for six days, and the weather cooperated for most of it.

We saw some beautiful mountain caribou, several black bears and some musk ox (mostly cows and calves). We attempted a lengthy stalk on a small herd but couldn't close the gap on the bulls. To our dismay and a drastic weather change, we were hauled off the mountain early. The helicopter pilot said we had a small window

of opportunity to get out due to loss of visibility (that, my friends, means a big snow storm). It was our only chance to get out for the next 7 to 10 days. Not taking any chances, we departed. Thankfully there was still time to plan another hunt.

The second adventure took place on Easter weekend 2012, which gave us only one week until the season ended. Mark and I flew in to Norman Wells again. We really lucked out on weather this trip. The week previous was −35°Celsius (C) during the day. For our week of hunting we got to enjoy days as warm as −3°C, and the night didn't get colder than −14°C—a welcomed relief as we were camping in a tent. On the afternoon of Friday, April 7, we set off by helicopter again to the Norman Range not far from where we had hunted in September. Flying in this time, we had clear blue skies, great visibility, and the pick of some great winter camping locations. We had a bird's eye view of the area and figured that we would have some decent hiking as the mountain tops were windswept. We were at the top of the mountain this hunting trip. We chose a nice camping spot that offered shelter from the elements and a nice spot for the chopper to drop us off where we wouldn't have to lug camp too far to set up.

After flying in, the law required we wait 12 hours before hunting, so we spent the first day setting up camp and getting settled in. We were lucky enough to have a great view that day while we set up camp—we kept an eye on five musk ox cows and calves on the next mountain over. We dug down into the snow about 3 feet to make a base for our tent, which would keep us nicely sheltered and warm. That evening while relaxing in our beautiful winter camp, we watched those five musk ox on the opposite side of the draw, approximately a kilometer away. It is unbelievable how light it stays in northern Canada—it stays light till about 10:45 P.M.—but we went to bed very early anyway. Though Mark did make me stay up till 8 o'clock.

On Saturday morning we got up to a crisp sunny day without a breath of wind. We had a light breakfast and saw that our neighbors, the five musk ox, were still on the next mountain. We started off spotting from camp, and to our delight two nice bulls showed themselves on a nearby mountain, approximately two kilometers away, so we prepared for our stalk.

The trek began as a decent hike through snow that was about a foot deep. We were making our way up to the windswept tops, which would allow for easy hiking. We made good time, but when we were about 30 minutes into our stalk, we were sure that we had been found out. Those two beautiful bulls were peering over the mountain top—the very one we were heading for. It appeared as if the two bulls were motionless and staring right at us. We stopped cold in our tracks, then very slowly made our way to what small

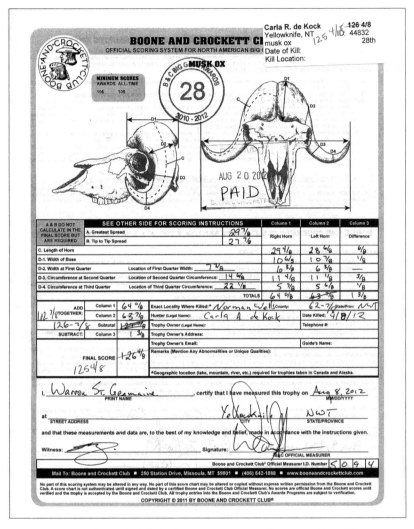

cover we had. I don't think they even got a glimpse of us. Those two bulls started facing each other; then, to our amazement, there was a musk ox brawl on the mountaintop. Each musk ox would back away from the other until they figured they were at a sufficient distance apart, and then they ran at each other and smashed horns. Due to the distance from where we were standing, it took several seconds for us to hear the clash. It was a ritual that they kept repeating. The force at which their heads made contact was incredible! They would make contact, shake their heads and then do it all over again. It was truly the most amazing sight! We watched for a while, then had to continue our stalk.

To remain out of sight, we had to rethink our plan of attack. That easy hike we had so hoped for was now out of the question. It looked like the new plan was a nice, easy hike in deep snow— sometimes waist- or chest-deep. Luckily for me, my trusty guide Mark was breaking trail. And luckily for him I packed my hiking poles along. Our stalk took about two hours of slogging through chest-deep snow.

As we got to about 200 yards from the musk ox, time was no longer relevant. My adrenaline was pumping—I was so happy to be up this close to not one but two shooters. From this point we had to belly crawl until we got to within about 70 yards. Luckily for me, that beautiful bull was standing broadside and I got off a shot. The first shot hit really hard but he just stood there looking shocked that something had struck him. Not wanting him to head down the backside of the mountain, I fired a second shot and he finally dropped. We let him settle for a bit and then went over to take a look at him. There he lay on the top of the mountain.

Then the work began. It took about five hours to field dress and debone. While we were field dressing my bull on the top of the mountain, we had an incredible view of a herd of approximately 25 musk ox on the next ridge.

My bull ended up scoring 125-6/8 points which makes it the second largest musk ox taken from Northwest Territories. It was a great experience to share with Mark, my guide and spouse.

Moose of a Lifetime

Robert J. Condon

Alaska-Yukon Moose | Current Rank #7

As told to Ted Forsi…

IN SEPTEMBER 2012, BOB CONDON, AN AVID VETERAN HUNTER from Soldotna, Alaska harvested one of the biggest bull moose ever! This is his story as told to Ted Forsi, one of many local hunters that have been really impressed with Bob and his good hunting fortunes.

CIRCA **2012**

Every year for the past 30 or 40 years, I looked forward to my annual moose-hunting trip in September. At my age, 73, I can't do as much physical hiking, packing and work around camp as I did when I was a youngster. Plus, on this trip, I was still regaining my strength from a heart attack and subsequent bypass surgery that I had about six months previous. My doctor told me I probably shouldn't be out moose hunting. I pondered this advice many times, but hunting is a big part of my life, and I really need to get out on a hunt every year.

For several years, my hunting partners and I traveled to the south slope of the Brooks Range for our hunt. This year, two close friends hunted with me; both have the same first name—Mike. I just refer to them as Old Mike and Young Mike! We spent several hours coordinating and planning our gear for the trip. They are great to have in camp and along for the hunt.

As with most hunts in Alaska, we booked an air taxi service to fly into a remote area to hunt. When planning a fly-in hunt, make sure you have a good checklist to ensure you have everything for a comfortable camp. This includes your camp, food and hunting gear. We planned ours for a 10-day hunt.

Between the three of us, we had two eight-man Cabela's Guide Model tents for our camp. We usually use one for sleeping and the second tent for cooking and storing our food. That way, when Mr. Grizzly comes by, hopefully the food will smell better to him than the three of us sweaty hunters, and he will attack the cook tent. Our food consisted mostly of freeze-dried meals so our total weight for the Beaver aircraft was within load limits.

We had our rifles in soft cases, binoculars, backpacks for packing meat, our propane cook stove and the rest of our miscellaneous camp and hunting gear. Good cold-weather clothing—gloves, hat and rain gear—is a must. We also took in light cots, sleeping pads and good sleeping bags—important for a good night's sleep while hunting.

Once we double-checked our gear list, we packed up and headed north to meet our air taxi. The fall had been a wet one here in Alaska with record rainfall. The air taxi operator suggested we rent a small raft from him to help cross the river where he was planning to drop us. At first we weren't sure if we needed it, but finally decided to spend a little extra cash and take it in with us. This decision proved to be a good one as we used this raft considerably during the hunt.

We set up camp on the shore of the river and settled in for our 10 days in the rugged, remote Alaskan wilderness. We pitched both tents and gathered some firewood. Since we couldn't hunt this first day, we did some glassing from camp and saw a few caribou moving through the area. We were also surprised to see two other hunters on a ridge above camp. We didn't know it then, but another air taxi had dropped them off downriver from our camp. We were a little disappointed to see other hunters nearby, but little did we know what a positive this would be for our hunt a little later.

After dinner we all hit the sleeping bags with a lot of anticipation for our first hunt the next day. At daylight the next morning we decided to stay close to camp where we could glass for a few miles in almost every direction. Shortly, the two other hunters we had seen the day before walked into our camp and introduced themselves. These guys were Luke and Dave Zirbel from Wisconsin and they turned out to be great guys. They told us they were camped about two miles downriver from us, had killed two big bulls and were in the process of packing the meat back to their camp. Being from Wisconsin, they only wanted to take the meat from one moose home with them and asked if we would like the meat from their second bull. We said yes.

They pointed out a hilltop about one mile away from our camp where they had done some glassing and had seen one other bull moose in the area. They thought it would be 50 inches or bigger. By current state hunting regulations, bull moose in this area have to be 50 inches wide or have four brow tines to be legal. They also said that they had left two camp chairs and their spotting scope on the hill, and we were welcome to use the chairs and scope if we wanted. Wow. This all sounded great to us! Young Mike and I decided to head up there that morning to glass. Old Mike decided to stay closer to camp and the river for his hunt.

We used the raft to cross the river. It was about a half a mile or so up the hill, and once there, we started glassing. It took me awhile to walk this distance as I was still feeling a little short of breath from my heart surgery. Young Mike was patient with me as I know he was raring to go.

We found the two camp chairs and had just settled in to start glassing. After about 15 minutes I thought I saw something moving about a mile or so away just inside a patch of spruce trees. Using my 10x40 Zeiss binoculars, I studied it, and it looked like a 4x8 sheet of plywood moving through the timber. I couldn't really believe my eyes, but it looked like a big bull moose.

Mike focused his binoculars on it and confirmed it was a bull moose. We were pretty sure it was 50 inches wide, but at that distance we really didn't know. The bull was quartering in our direction but at a very slow pace. I decided to use a lonely cow moose call to see if he was interested. He was. He started moving slowly in our direction and we thought about heading over to intercept it, but the country was very open and we were afraid he might see or wind us and head out.

Mike and I discussed what the best plan should be. I really wanted Mike to get a crack at his first bull moose. We decided that he would go back behind the hill, then do a wide circle to see if he could get into the edge of the timber where the bull looked like he was heading. I would do some bull and cow calls to see if I could interest him in closing the distance to Mike.

I couldn't really see where Mike was, but the moose was slowly closing the distance to me, and I was hoping Mike was getting within range of the bull.

At about 400 yards, he slowed his pace and finally stopped behind some alders and low willows. He actually turned around and went back about 75 yards. He was acting a bit suspicious and I wondered if he had gotten a stray scent from Mike or me. I gave another cow call and he turned and started coming back. I wasn't sure what to do and kept hoping Mike was in range of the bull.

The bull came back to about 350 yards of my position and stood there at full alert. I had seen bulls do this before and knew he was sizing up the situation. He was using his antlers, nose, and ears to try to figure out what was going on. I felt he was going to turn and leave and decided to get a good rest and take a shot. I knew that Mike was safely off to the left of the bull and not close to where I was going to shoot.

At this distance, it was obvious that he was a legal bull, and I thought he was in the 60- to 65-inch class. I found a small broken-

off tree that was perfect for a rest. I use a Browning A-Bolt .375 H&H Magnum with 270-grain bullets whenever I hunt in Alaska. I have a deep respect for these huge animals and want the firepower to put them down when I have the opportunity. I also have a deep respect for brown and grizzly bears and like to have the .375 with me when I hunt.

Using the rest over the broken tree, my first shot hit a little far back, but the bull just stood in the same place. So I followed up with a second shot, and the bull dropped. I waited a few minutes to make sure he was down for good and then walked over to the bull. When I got there I was shocked. The bull was a giant! I have taken several nice bulls over the years and most of them I estimated to be 1,100 to 1,200 pounds on the hoof. Just looking at this bull I felt he was more like 1,500 to 1,600 pounds. His antlers were much larger than I estimated, with great mass all the way from the bases to the ends of the palms.

About 5 minutes after I walked up to the bull, Mike gave a shout from about 200 yards away and asked, "Did you shoot something?"

I gave a yell back and said I got a bull. When he joined me, he couldn't believe it. From his location, he never saw the bull and really didn't know what had happened. At first he thought I had got a shot at a wolf or something else. I filled him in on what happened after he had left me, and he was just as excited as I was.

I just can't tell you how happy and humbled I was at the opportunity to harvest this fantastic bull. Mike and I took several photos and then got to work. Our other hunting partner Mike also came up to help, and the three of us quartered the bull and placed the meat in meat sacks to keep it as clean as possible. I decided to cape the bull for a full shoulder mount as this is probably my greatest hunting trophy ever.

The next morning, just before heading back for another load of meat, Luke and Dave came in with a load of their meat for us. We told them about my big bull and they offered to come up and help pack meat for us! In all my years of hunting I had never met two more generous hunters in the field.

Between the four of the young guys and me carrying my .375 for bear protection, we had all the meat packed into camp by late the second afternoon. Our last trip was to pack the antlers and cape back to camp. This was a major feat—we later weighed the antlers at 98 pounds, and I know the cape had to weigh at least 100 pounds. It took two of the guys to pack the antlers as they were so heavy and cumbersome.

Again, many thanks to Luke and Dave—especially after helping us pack meat for two days, they left our camp at night and still had to walk about two miles in the dark to return to their camp. These guys were gentlemen to the highest order!

That night I used our satellite phone to call my wife and tell her the good news. She was excited for us, but informed me that there was a big storm brewing out in the Bering Sea, and we might want to check with our air taxi to see if we could get some of the meat out early. I called the air taxi, and he said he would try to come in the next day to do a meat run. When he arrived, however, he said that we should consider coming out early since we already had the meat of two moose and the weather was going to turn really bad during the next day or so. I know from previous hunts that when the pilot says you should consider leaving early, it is probably a smart thing to do. We broke camp as fast as possible and loaded everything in the Beaver for our flight out.

Back in Soldotna I had a chance to get the bull scored for Boone and Crockett. The official score is 250-6/8 B&C points.

I can only say how humbled I feel at harvesting this great bull moose. I really can't put into words the respect I have for this old critter, and I am just so happy to have had a chance to experience another moose hunt in Alaska. I also want to say another special thanks to my hunting partners and new friends Luke and Dave for all of their help to make this hunt a memory that will last forever.

Now if my health holds out, maybe next year we can do it again!

PRIZE WINNING TROPHIES
Submitted for the
1950 NORTH AMERICAN
BIG GAME COMPETITION
of the
BOONE AND CROCKETT CLUB

Science Behind Keeping Records

Justin Spring

B&C Assistant Director of Big Game Records

BOONE AND CROCKETT CLUB'S RECORDS-KEEPING SYSTEM DATES back to 1949 when a Boone and Crockett Club committee was tasked with developing a scoring method to rank North American trophies. Prior to that, trophies were recorded and the top entries were invited to a competition, but the judging was highly subjective. While this was appropriate during a time of very few mature specimens, as wildlife populations began to rebound, it became readily apparent that records must be standardized if they were to remain relevant in the battle for wildlife conservation.

The system implemented in 1950 is still used today by B&C, along with a very long list of other national groups from the Pope and Young Club to dozens of state scoring associations across the country. While it's enjoyable to compare trophies with hunting companions, the basis of this system lies in the recording of mature specimens from all categories of native North American big game. The idea of recording only mature males taken within the rules of fair chase is twofold. First, it incentivizes hunters to be selective and to ensure their take is not leading to the overconsumption of the resource.

Selective hunting takes pressure off immature and female members of the species—which, at the time the system was developed, was paramount to facilitating the recovery of North American big game. The second is the promotion of an ethic to which hunters could hold themselves accountable, ensuring consumption of the resource is not overindulgent.

Several questions arose as B&C established a set of rules to help guide hunter preference. How do we gauge wildlife populations through the data collected through our records? What do the details of the measurements take into account, and how is the data useful?

The idea of records keeping and the reason we continue their collection today is their use as a data set of all North American big game. Nearly all agencies keep records of population estimates, hunter densites, etc. While this data is useful in state management, it does not provide a snapshot of the entire continent's game populations. Realizing this is the goal of Boone and Crockett Club, the question becomes, *How do you keep a data set to gauge populations of 32 big game species across an area of over 9.5 million square miles?* Herein lies the part of the system that is most greatly misunderstood. If we gauge trophies that have passed their prime breeding age and exhibit certain characteristics of a very mature animal, we can gauge wildlife health on a continental scale. We can identify regions of the continent either succeeding or failing by comparing entry rates with hunter numbers and availability. This threshold of mature specimens exhibiting only the strongest normal traits of the species is where B&C sets its minimum scores for each category. While you would never think so by observing outdoor media today, a typical whitetail deer scoring 160 inches carries just as much value as a data point as the next World's Record. People get so hung up on the abnormal and final number, they lose sight of the score as a measure of wildlife population health and not that of their prowess as a hunter.

For example, a typical whitetail deer, to be considered a prime, mature animal, must exhibit antlers with 160 inches of mass, beam lengths, tine lengths, and spread. In order for this to happen, the deer must be allowed not only the minimum requirements for survival, but also additional nutrition and prime habitat to exhibit that 160 inches of antler. Antlers are a secondary sexual characteristic, meaning they are expressed in males to show their reproductive value and to compete for breeding rights. Antlers develop after survival requirements are met. For this to be achieved, the specimen must have all the required nutrient intake, mineral availability, habitat suitability, and so on. A buck will be unable to reach the minimum score if an area has an overpopulation of deer and/or browse is limited—and therefore, the nutrition to create additional antler is not available. If an area produces none or very few mature specimens, this points to a habitat or population problem and is cause for further investigation.

Some variations in entry rates are easily explainable. If you look at the upper Midwest, there appears to be a good gradient that in most cases does not halt at a state line. Should this happen, it would suggest that perhaps the state where the density increases or decreases is doing something differently to manage the game. State lines are arbitrary boundaries created by humans and variations in trophy density between neighboring states are nearly always attributed to differing management strategies.

Examining historical versus more recent data can also be used in gauging herd health and also gauging effects of major changes such as illegal harvest, changing predator management regulations, or an increase or decrease in tag numbers.

While most species are doing well, there are a few that are not; for example, the various caribou species. There are some successes and failures, but overall trophy entries are down. Lowering the minimum entry score has been discussed, although this creates a false sense of quality habitat. If caribou used to be larger, we must not resign ourselves to smaller caribou; instead we should throw our resources at discovering what is causing population declines. We see mountain caribou still doing well. It is mainly the migratory herds that we are seeing drop in numbers of trophy entries. Without

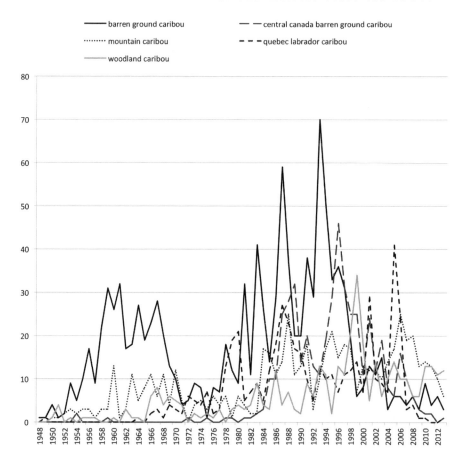

Caribou Entries since the 1940s

a national comparison, individual investigations into the decline in particular areas may miss this fact or others that the scientific community has yet to identify.

A second interesting analysis is that of the whitetail. After decades of continual increases we finally peaked and saw major declines across the country in the 2013 season. Every year, deer shows in Iowa, Illinois, and Wisconsin display the top heads from the year's hunt. All of them were down in trophies. Each individual state could point to management failure, predation, or a laundry list of other factors, but only B&C has the data to do an in-depth analysis of whitetails across their entire range. Midway through the calendar year, the drop is slightly exaggerated since we usually receive entries through the following season, but something happened on a national scale that dropped entries significantly. This decrease is being investigated on numerous levels, and the conclusions are yet to be formulated. However, I hope you can see by now that our data set is maintained specifically for this type of analysis.

Boone and Crockett Club's records program is always trying to expand the data we collect in order to produce a more viable data set for both wildlife managers and sportsmen as well as other wildlife enthusiasts. Our most recent undertakings involve a ramped-up effort to obtain trophy age data. For some species such as the bighorn sheep, trophies are aged by experienced biologists when they are checked in after harvest. This gives us the ability to analyze age versus score in different regions. If a particular area produces 190-inch bighorns at age 6, such as the Missouri Breaks, or it takes 10-plus years to reach that maturity, as we commonly see in Alberta, we can compare habitats and see what factors allow this excessive growth at a young age not seen in other locations.

While this may be interesting for a hunter selecting a location to pursue bighorns, it has much further-reaching consequences. A study was completed in Canada where they documented a decrease in horn size relative to the age of the rams harvested. This was ultimately attributed to hunter selection. This particular area has a ram mortality of 100 percent once they reach legal minimum size. It is a very small, isolated population that is extremely accessible with no limit on tags. I don't foresee this example taking place in most sheep populations—as harvest is extremely limited and highly monitored—though it showed that under intense harvest, mean horn size decreased.

The question becomes, *Are other areas experiencing this side effect of trophy selection?* The only way to truthfully sort this out is to put together a strong age data set. If an area produced elk that scored 375

Whitetail Deer Entries since 1995

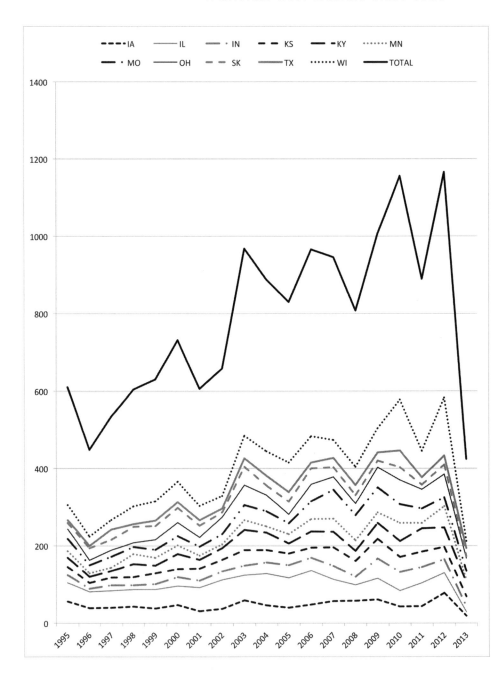

points at age 7 and now they don't reach 360 points until age 9, we know that population health or habitat quality has degraded. Other contributing factors could include predation, which can prevent animals from consuming and converting nutrients to antler, as well as hunters altering selection by harvesting the larger trophies at a level that pushes smaller bulls that produce smaller racks into the main breeding position. The way to determine if this is the case is to attach an age to the antler or horn score. As hunters, we do not want to harm a population or alter genetic selection; rather, harvest the surplus for our use while allowing the species to thrive.

This idea that the records data are for wildlife health and not the hunter's ego is the most important aspect to stress when explaining why we keep records. Records are maintained as a tool to gauge wildlife management successes and failures. In order to create successful estimates, we must receive a high portion of qualifying trophies—be it picked-up heads or trophies taken by any means from archery to rifle, or road kills. In order for this data set to be valid, it falls to the hunter to enter his or her trophy to ensure the opportunities we are afforded today are there for future generations.

The next time you are sitting around camp and a hunting buddy starts in about all the records book-qualifying heads he has but doesn't care about the score, inform him of the purpose of the records: it has nothing to do with chest pounding and everything to do with species conservation. There isn't a hunter out there who thinks the wildlife management authority in charge of their particular area is not making mistakes. B&C records are a way to call hunters to task on this. This is the dataset completed by people on the ground; these are the results of public hunting of public wildlife ensured through the North American Model for Wildlife Conservation. These records are the report cards for which we all must be held accountable regardless of our personal selection or desire to be listed in "the book."

Acknowledgments

Big Trophies, Epic Hunts
True Tales of Self-Guided Adventure from the
Boone and Crockett Club

WE WOULD LIKE TO THANK ALL THE B&C OFFICIAL MEASURERS who have volunteered thousands of hours scoring North American big game animals for the sportsmen across our great continent. Their work is integral in providing the scientific data B&C's Big Game Records Department needs to make our work as complete as possible.

We would also like to thank B&C Official Measurer and Lifetime Associate Hanspeter Giger for his continued support and contributions to our publishing program. He spent countless hours researching the Sagamore Hill Award winners and compiling an engaging chapter for this book, including scoring notes for each trophy. Hanspeter also studied all of the Club's Awards books in search of stories that would fit the criteria for this publication. The book wouldn't have been possible without his help.

Additional assistance provided by B&C staff members, in particular: Wendy Nickelson, Justin Spring, Karlie Slayer, Mark Mesenko, and Abra Loran.

DESIGN AND PRODUCTION
Julie L. Tripp – B&C Director of Publications

COVER PHOTOGRAPH
Denver Bryan – Images on the Wildside

PRINTED IN THE U.S.
Edward Brothers Malloy – Lillington, North Carolina